How to access the supplemental web resource

We are pleased to provide access to a web resource that supplements your textbook, *Beginning Musical Theatre Dance*. This resource offers extended learning activities, e-journal prompts, chapter quizzes, web links, and more.

Accessing the web resource is easy!
Follow these steps if you purchased a new book:

1. Visit **www.HumanKinetics.com/BeginningMusicalTheatreDance**.

2. Click the <u>first edition</u> link next to the book cover.

3. Click the Sign In link on the left or top of the page. If you do not have an account with Human Kinetics, you will be prompted to create one.

4. If the online product you purchased does not appear in the Ancillary Items box on the left of the page, click the Enter Key Code option in that box. Enter the key code that is printed at the right, including all hyphens. Click the Submit button to unlock your online product.

5. After you have entered your key code the first time, you will never have to enter it again to access this product. Once unlocked, a link to your product will permanently appear in the menu on the left. For future visits, all you need to do is sign in to the textbook's website and follow the link that appears in the left menu!

→ Click the Need Help? button on the textbook's website if you need assistance along the way.

How to access the web resource if you purchased a used book:

You may purchase access to the web resource by visiting the text's website, **www.HumanKinetics.com/BeginningMusicalTheatreDance**, or by calling the following:

800-747-4457 . . . . U.S. customers
800-465-7301 . . . . Canadian customers
+44 (0) 113 255 5665 . . . . European customers
08 8372 0999 . . . . Australian customers
0800 222 062 . . . . New Zealand customers
217-351-5076 . . . . International customers

For technical support, send an e-mail to:
support@hkusa.com . . . . U.S. and international customers
info@hkcanada.com . . . . Canadian customers
academic@hkeurope.com . . . . European customers
keycodesupport@hkaustralia.com . . . . Australian and New Zealand customers

HUMAN KINETICS
The Information Leader in Physical Activity &

D0303208

Product: Beginning Musical Theatre Dance web resource

Key code: HARRIS-UPWEHQ-OSG

This unique code allows you access to the web resource.

Access is provided if you have purchased a new book. Once submitted, the code may not be entered for any other user.

Beginning
MUSICAL THEATRE
DANCE

INTERACTIVE DANCE SERIES

Diana Dart Harris

Human Kinetics

Library of Congress Cataloging-in-Publication Data

Harris, Diana Dart, 1969-
 Beginning musical theatre dance / Diana Dart Harris
    pages cm. -- (Interactive Dance Series)
 Includes webography.
 Includes bibliographical references and index.
1. Dance--Study and teaching. 2. Musicals. 3. Musical theater. 4. Performing arts. I. Title.
 GV1589.H37 2015
 793.307--dc23
                           2015007826

ISBN: 978-1-4925-0289-0 (print)

The web addresses cited in this text were current as of August 2015, unless otherwise noted.

Acquisitions Editor: Gayle Kassing, PhD; **Developmental Editor:** Bethany J. Bentley; **Managing Editor:** Derek Campbell; **Copyeditor:** Bob Replinger **Indexer:** Nancy Ball; **Permissions Manager:** Dalene Reeder; **Graphic Designers:** Joe Buck and Tara Welsch; **Cover Designer:** Keith Blomberg; **Photographer (cover and interior):** Bernard Wolff; photographs © Human Kinetics unless otherwise noted; photo on p. 85 courtesy of the Barnard Archives and Special Collections, Barnard College; photo on p. 86 courtesy of the Library of Congress/ Imre Kiralfy; photos on pp. 88 and 90 © Photofest; photo on p. 92 © Photofest, photographer Maurice Seymour; photo on p. 94 © Universal Pictures/Photofest; photo on p. 113 courtesy of Mags DePetris; **Photo Asset Manager:** Laura Fitch; **Visual Production Assistant:** Joyce Brumfield; **Photo Production Manager:** Jason Allen; **Art Manager:** Kelly Hendren; **Associate Art Manager:** Alan L. Wilborn; **Illustrations:** © Human Kinetics; **Printer:** Versa Press

We thank Parkland College in Champaign, Illinois, for assistance in providing the location for the photo shoot for this book.

The video contents of this product are licensed for educational public performance for viewing by a traditional (live) audience, via closed circuit television, or via computerized local area networks within a single building or geographically unified campus. To request a license to broadcast these contents to a wider audience—for example, throughout a school district or state, or on a television station—please contact your sales representative (www. HumanKinetics.com/SalesRepresentatives).

Printed in the United States of America   10 9 8 7 6 5 4 3 2 1

The paper in this book is certified under a sustainable forestry program.

Human Kinetics
Website: www.HumanKinetics.com

United States: Human Kinetics
P.O. Box 5076
Champaign, IL 61825-5076
800-747-4457
e-mail: info@hkusa.com

Canada: Human Kinetics
475 Devonshire Road Unit 100
Windsor, ON N8Y 2L5
800-465-7301 (in Canada only)
e-mail: info@hkcanada.com

Europe: Human Kinetics
107 Bradford Road
Stanningley
Leeds LS28 6AT, United Kingdom
+44 (0) 113 255 5665
e-mail: hk@hkeurope.com

Australia: Human Kinetics
57A Price Avenue
Lower Mitcham, South Australia 5062
08 8372 0999
e-mail: info@hkaustralia.com

New Zealand: Human Kinetics
P.O. Box 80
Mitcham Shopping Centre, South Australia 5062
0800 222 062
e-mail: info@hknewzealand.com

E6394

This book is dedicated to all of my students—my past students who have been my teachers as well as students, my current students who fuel my passion each day, and my future students who will provide me the opportunity to continue to use dance to make a difference.

Contents

Preface

Musical theatre dance is a genre that includes all types of dance. Dancers who perform in musicals must be able to adapt to whatever form of dance the choreographer demands, whether it be ballet, modern, jazz, hip-hop, contemporary, ballroom, folk, or ethnic dance. Many high schools perform annual musicals, and some compete on a national level. Dance departments at colleges and universities annually audition hundreds of students who want to be a part of their musical theatre programs.

Dancers learn the specific techniques and styles that they may need to perform in shows, but unless they have experience performing, the practical side of musical theatre dance is often severely neglected. Dancers often have to learn how theatre works after they have already auditioned, been hired, and are in the throes of production rehearsals.

Performing on the musical theatre stage is an opportunity unlike any other a trained dancer will experience. Musical theatre dancers need to follow and respect theatrical traditions, become familiar with working terminology, and gain general knowledge of how a musical is produced.

This book will provide you with practical information, as well as historical background, about musical theatre dance. Although it is intended for high school and college students who are beginning to explore the path to performing on a musical theatre stage, those interested in learning about what it takes to be a dancer on the musical theatre stage will find both general theatre information and specific dance information in this textbook.

Chapter 1 introduces musical theatre dance. Besides providing a working definition, it will help you understand what makes performing on a musical theatre stage a different and unique experience for dancers. In chapter 2 you will learn how to prepare for class. Chapter 3 gives you details on dancer health and wellness and will teach you how to care for your body when the physical demands of taking part in a production may become overwhelming. An overview of the body's anatomy, including how joints, muscles, tendons, and ligaments work together to shape the dances seen on the stage, is provided to help you develop body awareness and promote injury prevention. Information is also provided about the importance of both warming up and cooling down the body before and after a rehearsal or performance and caring for an injury should one occur. Additionally, you will learn the importance of proper nutrition and hydration during rehearsals and performances.

Chapters 4 through 6 tell you how to apply this general knowledge to specific situations. Chapter 4 introduces and defines dance terminology used on the musical theatre stage, and chapter 5 offers descriptions of steps commonly used in musical theatre dance. Chapter 6 includes details about how to audition and what you can expect, expected behavior at rehearsals and during the run of a performance, theatrical etiquette, and the roles of dancers and choreographers in a production.

The final chapter takes you on a historical journey beginning with Greek dramas and tracing the roots of dance through minstrelsy, vaudeville, and the eras of dance directors and choreographers. It concludes with information on integration musicals, concept musicals, and today's dance musicals.

The web resource that accompanies this book offers supplemental interactive instruction. Visit **www.HumanKinetics.com/BeginningMusicalTheatreDance** to check it out. The web resource provides you with added opportunities to practice the steps described in this book. You will also find handouts, worksheets, quizzes, and more.

Musical theatre dance is a specialized genre of performance dance that requires all the training of a dancer combined with an understanding of how to tell a character's story through movement. Working in a new environment that is foreign in many ways can be challenging if you have never performed in musical theatre before. If you arrive armed with the knowledge of how the world of musical theatre works, what the expectations are, and how to audition, rehearse, perform, and care for yourself, you will have the power to be successful. You will be able to fulfill your dream of successfully dancing on the musical theatre stage while respecting the rich history of musical theatre and helping define its future.

eBook available at your campus bookstore or HumanKinetics.com

Acknowledgments

Special thanks to Shannon Bogucki Cushing, who originally encouraged me to begin writing for dancers. Thank you also to my husband, Mark, and my children for their support, love, and patience while I was writing; my mother for introducing me to dance and keeping me involved in it; my father for constantly encouraging me to write; and Keith Luckenbach for his high expectations and guidance in shaping my writing. I would also like to thank everyone at Human Kinetics who made this experience a pleasant one, especially my editors, Gayle Kassing and Bethany Bentley, for guiding me on this journey.

How to Use the Web Resource

In a musical theatre dance class, steps and combinations can move quickly. They can contain a large number of new movements or small additions to movements you have already learned. But you have an advantage! Your personal tutor is just a few clicks away and always available to help you remember and practice the steps learned in class. You can study between class meetings or when you are doing mental practice to memorize exercises or movement. Check out the web resource that accompanies the book at **www.HumanKinetics.com/BeginningMusicalTheatreDance**.

The web resource is an interactive tool that you can use to enhance your understanding of beginning musical theatre dance technique, review what you studied in class, or prepare for performance testing. It contains information about each step, including notes for correct performance; photos of foot and arm positions; and video clips of musical theatre dance techniques. Also included are interactive quizzes for each chapter of the *Beginning Musical Theatre Dance* text, which let you test your knowledge of concepts, musical theatre dance basics, terminology, and more.

In a beginning musical theatre dance class, students learn about technique, musical theatre dance as an art form, and themselves. The supplementary materials section of the web resource contains the following additional components for each chapter of the *Beginning Musical Theatre Dance* text. These components support both learning in the musical theatre dance class and exploring more about the world of musical theatre dance.

- Glossary terms from the text are presented so that you can check your knowledge of the translated meaning of the term as well as a description of the term.
- Web links give you a starting place to learn more about musical theatre dance techniques, styles, and dance companies.
- Chapters include e-journaling prompts, handouts, and assignments that will help you think more deeply about beginning musical theatre dance class.
- Other assignments include specific activities to apply concepts and ideas about musical theatre dance.

We hope that the web resource helps you individualize your learning experience so that you can connect to, expand, and apply your learning of beginning musical theatre dance, enhancing your success and enjoyment in your study of this dance genre.

Chapter 1

Introduction to Musical Theatre Dance

The stage manager calls, "Five minutes, please," and from every dressing room comes the response, "Five minutes, thank you!" Final touches are put on costumes, makeup and hair are checked, and actors begin to make their way toward the stage. Soon the stage manager will call for places, and everything that has led up to this point will be forgotten. No one will be thinking about the arduous and nerve-wracking audition process, no one will be remembering the long hours of rehearsals, and no one will be counting the years of training that led to this moment. The actors will hear the first notes of the orchestra, watch the curtain open, feel the warmth of the lights, and sense the excitement of an expectant audience. For a few hours, they will transport that audience to a place where spoken words become songs and every movement is part of a dance.

DEFINING MUSICAL THEATRE DANCE

Musical theatre dance is a broad term that includes any form of dance, movement, or dance scene used in combination with singing and acting to help tell a story. As a musical theatre dancer, you will be trained in a variety of dance forms and styles to ensure that you are able to perform whatever type of dance a choreographer chooses to create. Some shows may require folk dance, others may require jazz or tap dance, and still other shows may simply require stylized gestures and movements that do not fit into any particular category but require the grace and strength of a trained dancer.

Musical theatre dances are part of a bigger picture. They are not designed to stand on their own and entertain audiences independently, although some can. These dances are choreographed to further an audience's understanding of a play through movement. For that to occur, musical theatre dancers need to be more than just dancers.

UNIQUE FEATURES OF MUSICAL THEATRE DANCE

Musical theatre dance is a unique genre of dance. Simply learning to dance and perform is not enough. As a musical theatre dancer, you will have to meet high expectations to be successful. You will have to train in a variety of dance forms and styles and to receive training in singing and acting. Additionally, you will need to learn how to adapt your dancing to accommodate props, scenery, costumes, and various types of musical accompaniment.

Performing a Variety of Dance Forms and Styles

Many dancers begin their training by being exposed to several genres of dance and then choosing one or two to study in depth. These dancers may eventually join companies that focus on a particular form or style. As a musical theatre dancer, you must be trained in many forms of dance and will need to be able to perform them well. The hundreds of musicals that have been written span many historical periods. Some may require cultural or folk dancing; others may require ballet, jazz, tap, or modern dance; and still others may require several forms of dance within the same production. You will have the opportunity to become versed in many forms and styles. The wider the variety of your technical training is, the more marketable you become. Studying any form of dance requires a financial commitment. Besides purchasing dance attire, you will have to purchase various types of shoes. Some shows may require ballet slippers, whereas others may require jazz oxfords, character shoes, or tap shoes.

Being a Triple-Threat Performer

A **triple-threat** performer is someone who is able to sing, act, and dance well. Simply having training in each of these areas is not enough. You have to continue to act like your character while performing **choreography**, and unless an instrumental dance break occurs in the music, you will be required to sing while you are dancing.

In the 1930s and 1940s musical theatre productions morphed into **integration musicals**. Before then, productions were similar to variety shows that included musical acts and dance acts. Companies often had the luxury of hiring a group of singers who provided the musical portion of a play and a separate group of dancers to perform the show's choreography. This practice was expensive because a large number of people had to be hired for each show and separate rehearsals were required. Integration musicals changed all that. Choreographers no longer worked alone; they were asked to integrate the music and the dance to tell a complete story.

Therefore, you will need to know how to combine all three skills effectively. A choreographed dance in a musical will likely be used to tell a story within a story, help the audience understand what is happening, or help move the plot line along. Dances are not included simply to entertain or foster an appreciation for the art of dance. Every time you step onto the stage, you will be charged with the task of capturing and holding the audience's attention while helping them understand the story.

DID YOU KNOW?

Musical theatre dancers must learn how to dance and sing at the same time. Dance alone requires an increase in oxygen intake for the body to meet its demands. Dancers must learn how to pace their dancing and when to take time to breathe. When dancers have to move and sing at the same time, they must learn how to move efficiently and how to breathe so that they can perform the physical movements without sacrificing volume or pitch while singing.

Performing With Costumes, Props, and Scenery

Dancing in a musical theatre setting is a different experience from performing in a dance company or in a traditional dance performance. You will be expected to answer to a **director**, a **music director**, and a **choreographer**. You must learn to dance in costumes that are appropriate for a particular role but may make dancing more challenging, you must learn to adjust choreography to accommodate scenery, and you will have to work with props.

Rarely in musical theatre will dancers be able to use the entire stage freely. Dancers usually have to dance around sets, in front of drops, or in a particular area of the stage. As a result, you will gain greater **spatial awareness**. You will have to be flexible enough to change what you are doing at any point in time. Many times a choreographed dance must be changed or reshaped when the dancers move into the theatre. You will have to learn to be attentive and to apply these changes immediately.

Props often add visual, dynamic interest to musical theatre dances.

Musical Challenges

Another unique aspect of musical theatre dancing is understanding different types of music and being able to adapt to various forms of musical accompaniment. Productions may call for different types of music ranging from big band to ethnic songs. Dancers often dance to recorded music or simple piano accompaniment during much of the rehearsal process. When technical and dress rehearsals begin, a complete orchestra of live musicians will be playing the music. The music may sound different, and the tempo, or speed, of songs may be different for the dancers. The experience of working with live musicians is exciting, but it can be challenging for the dancers, who must learn to listen and adapt to those changes.

TYPES OF MUSICAL THEATRE

Musical theatre dance training can begin at any age, and dancers will have many opportunities to perform. Many middle schools now present junior versions of popular musicals. Selections from musicals or complete musical productions are performed as culminating activities in both high school and college theatrical classes. Theatre or music departments in high schools and colleges often produce annual musicals that offer musical theatre dance students an opportunity to perform.

After studying musical theatre dance, you may audition to perform professionally. Recognize, however, that the professional theatrical world is competitive. A tiny percentage of dancers are hired to be part of a Broadway production. Another possibility is to audition for a touring company. These companies offer an experience similar to that of a Broadway show while providing a chance for travel. Other options include auditioning for movie musicals and commercials.

You may choose not to perform professionally but find that you have a love for musical theatre and a desire to perform. Regional companies and community theatre groups often hold auditions for trained actors, musicians, singers, and dancers who have chosen other careers.

BENEFITS OF STUDYING MUSICAL THEATRE DANCE

Musical theatre dance training can be beneficial on a physical level, an intellectual level, and an emotional level.

Musical theatre dancers benefit physically in many ways. You will develop muscular strength and flexibility and be able to move quickly and efficiently. Additionally, dance can improve the efficiency of your body's systems. Dancers' bodies have circulatory and respiratory systems that are able to circulate blood efficiently and deliver oxygen to cells quickly. Dance requires movements that help to establish new pathways within the nervous system. In turn, these pathways improve communication between the brain and the body's muscles. Dancers' bodies often metabolize food quickly, meaning that they can rapidly and efficiently convert food to fuel for the muscles to use.

Early in the audition process, as a musical theatre dancer, you will learn how to deal with what life throws your way and develop ways of coping with disappointment and anxiety. Dancers who audition for musicals are a dime a dozen. The field is competitive. You will likely learn how to deal with rejection early in your career, and you will have to attend many auditions before you earn a spot in a show. You will also learn to persevere in spite of failing and will come to understand that hard work is just as important as talent in the theatrical world.

Musical theatre dancers also develop artistic literacy. Although anyone can read and gather information on musical theatre dancing, singing, and acting, training in musical theatre is practical and experiential. You are trained to use the four fundamental practices of imagination, investigation, construction, and reflection.

You will learn to do research, use your imagination, construct characters, and reflect on your art form. Unlike other types of dancers, who might be given choreography and simply told to perform it, you will have the job of using choreography to tell a story to an audience that is often composed of people of a variety of ages and backgrounds who may not know much at all about dance. You will need to do research and develop your character, and then you will be charged with using your creativity and imagination to perform choreography in a way that is consistent with the personalities of your unique characters.

Even if your intent is not to perform professionally, studying musical theatre dance and performing in a production will provide you with skills that are useful in life. You will learn the importance of discipline, dedication, responsibility, and commitment to yourself and others.

Learning all this will encourage you to take pride in yourself. The audition process will teach you how to present yourself to others. In today's world where most contact is made electronically, you will have the opportunity to develop your skills of personal contact.

You will also learn about all the aspects of the theatre. This learning will help you develop an appreciation for all the work that goes into producing a musical. You may not always be a performer, but the learned appreciation may encourage you to pursue other careers in the theatre such as stage management or arts administration.

Whether or not you work in the theatre, you may become an audience member or a theatrical philanthropist who will support theatre. By having a positive experience, you will likely want to help give others the same opportunities by contributing to future productions in some way.

BASICS OF MUSICAL THEATRE DANCE CLASS

You will benefit by knowing what to expect when you walk into a musical theatre dance class. A dance studio is different from other types of classrooms, and the relationship between the teacher and the students is different as well.

Physical Environment

Your class may take place in a dedicated dance studio or in a room that has many purposes. The room may have metal or wooden railings, called barres, that are either attached to the walls or are portable and can stand alone. The room may have mirrors lining one wall. The mirrors help your teacher see everyone in the room and allow you and your teacher to see your line and posture. Although the mirrors may seem intimidating at first, you will quickly become accustomed to using them to learn. Dance studios usually have wooden or vinyl floors that offer shock absorption when you land from jumps. Some dance classes are taught in gyms or auditoriums that have no barres or mirrors.

SAFETY TIP

As a musical theatre dancer, you will have to learn how to dance in many types of shoes. You should always rehearse in the type of shoe you will be performing in so that you grow accustomed to how a shoe can change the way you move and change your center of gravity. Making these adjustments right away can be difficult. When changing from one type of shoe to another during a class or rehearsal, you should walk around a bit in the shoe to give your body time to adjust before jumping right into a dance sequence.

Role of the Teacher

Dance teachers are emissaries of the art form. Your teacher's personal experience and perspective will influence how the class is organized and how information is passed on. But you can expect that learning choreography from various musicals will be part of any musical theatre dance class.

At some point during your musical theatre dance class, your teacher will give you feedback or constructive criticism. This feedback may be in the form of comments to the entire class or comments directed specifically at you. You should take any constructive criticism as a compliment. These comments mean that the teacher sees potential in you and wants to encourage you to grow in your dancing and become the best musical theatre dance artist you can be.

Role of the Student

Students in musical theatre dance have responsibilities toward themselves. The first is to participate as fully as possible. Although some movements may be unfamiliar, you will make little progress in technique without your full physical and mental participation. You should always pay careful attention to everything the teacher does and says. Dance is an art form learned primarily through careful observation and listening.

> **DID YOU KNOW?**
>
> Dances are usually taught in 8-count phrases. A teacher or choreographer will often put together four of these phrases in a 32-count block and teach the dances in these 32-count blocks.

EXPECTATIONS FOR STUDENTS

Like all classes, dance classes come with rules and expectations. Most of the rules of the dance studio are steeped in tradition and create a code of dance etiquette that should be followed in all dance classes.

Attending Class Consistently

Like dancers in every dance genre, musical theatre dance students are expected to attend all classes and rehearsals. Because musical theatre dancers must be trained

Fully participating in exercises will help ensure your success.

in a variety of forms and styles, missing even a few classes can be detrimental. Teachers must expose the students to many forms of dance in a short time. Absences mean that you may miss learning particular ones and will thus be unprepared to audition for shows that require those forms of dance.

Preparing and Practicing

Class time is spent learning different forms of dance and then learning choreography based in those forms. Often, the choreography is taught over the course of several class meetings. You will be expected to learn the choreography in class and practice it at home so that new material or additional choreography can be taught during the following class.

STRUCTURE OF MUSICAL THEATRE DANCE CLASS

The goal of musical theatre dance classes is to teach the students steps, combinations, or dances from a particular musical. The form of dance that is used in the musical will determine what type of class is taught. Although all classes will start with a complete body warm-up, the form of the combination will determine whether the warm-up is based in ballet, tap, jazz, modern, folk, or cultural dance.

The warm-up will be followed by the teaching of individual steps that will be part of the culminating combination. These steps may be taught in the center of the floor or in lines traveling across the dance floor.

The last third of the class will be focused on learning the chosen choreography. You will learn the combination in a large group as a class and then be broken down into smaller groups to have a chance to perform it. Breaking down into smaller groups serves two purposes: It gives other dancers a chance to see the choreography being performed, and it gives the dancers more space to use as they perform. It is customary to applaud for each small group as the dancers perform.

At the conclusion of every class, you will be expected to walk up to the teacher and verbally thank him or her before you leave the studio.

Musical theatre dance is a challenging genre because it involves learning a variety of dance forms and styles. Additionally, you will need to study voice and acting and to combine all three of these skills to be a successful performer. Knowing what to expect will help you rise to this challenge. You will have many opportunities to use these skills. As long as you understand the expectations of studying this genre of dance and come to class prepared, you will learn an enormous amount about dance and have an enjoyable experience.

SUMMARY

Musical theatre dance is an exciting and unique field that offers you the opportunity to use your dance skills while learning others. The training requires discipline, dedication, and hard work, but you will have many opportunities to perform.

Professional, regional, and community theatre groups all provide chances for you to perform while continuing to learn about the workings of the theatre. Additionally, studying musical theatre dance provides you with skills and qualities that will help you live a successful life.

To find supplementary materials for this chapter, such as learning activities, e-journal assignments, and web links, visit the web resource at www.HumanKinetics.com/BeginningMusicalTheatreDance.

Chapter 2

Preparing for Class

Walking into a musical theatre dance class for the first time can be exciting, but it can also be overwhelming if you do not know what to expect or if you are unprepared. Being prepared means knowing what to wear for class and what to bring with you, as well as being prepared both physically and mentally.

DRESSING FOR CLASS

Clothing requirements for musical theatre dance vary depending on the instructor, who normally discusses this subject during the first class. Clothing should be nonrestrictive and allow movement in all directions. In addition, it should be form fitting so that the teacher can see your body to check for proper positioning.

Traditional Attire

Some instructors may take a traditional approach and require leotards and tights. Leotards are made of a spandex cotton blend and come in many colors and styles. Unless a teacher has a specific requirement, you can choose the color or print you prefer. Leotards come in scoop neck, V-neck, sleeveless, short-sleeve, and long-sleeve styles. You should choose a style that offers personal comfort and is suitable for the temperature of the studio.

Dance tights are made of nylon and spandex. Thicker than fashion tights, they are designed to endure all the stretching that dance movements require. They will also stand up to repeated washings. Dance tights are designed so that dancers need not wear underwear with them. Underwear may bunch up, stick out, or cause unnecessary lines. Tights also come in various colors or styles. Black and suntan tights are usually the choices for musical theatre dance class.

You will have the option of purchasing footed tights, footless tights, or convertible tights. Convertible tights have an opening at the bottom of each foot so that they can be pulled down over your feet or folded up around your ankles. Convertible tights are the most practical for musical theatre dance because they can be rolled up should you need to dance barefoot or used to cover your feet when you must wear shoes.

Contemporary Attire

Some instructors may take a contemporary approach regarding attire. Instead of tights, dancers may wear jazz pants or bike pants with a leotard. Other teachers may allow students to wear a tank top or T-shirt. Another option is a unitard, a one-piece outfit made of the same material as a leotard that covers the legs and the torso.

Undergarments

Females should invest in a dance bra or sports bra to wear under a leotard or shirt. Made of a cotton spandex blend, these bras fit tighter than normal bras and provide the extra support needed during physical activity.

Males should wear a dance belt, the traditional undergarment for males, to provide necessary support. Although similar to an athletic supporter, a dance belt is designed specifically for dance.

Because dancers perspire during class, practice clothes should be washed after every wearing. You should probably have more than one outfit, especially if a class meets several times a week.

Hair

Your hair should always be pulled back and away from the face during class. Loose hair can be distracting to both you and your teacher. Although pulling the hair into a ponytail is usually sufficient, if you have extremely long hair you might choose to gather the ponytail with a clip or into a bun. Securing the hair is especially helpful when you are practicing turns and have to move your head quickly.

SAFETY TIP

Leaving your jewelry at home is best. You should not wear bracelets, watches, or necklaces because they can move around and injure you. Jewelry may also hurt another dancer should a collision occur or should it fly off and hit someone. Although stud earrings are acceptable, you should remove any type of hanging earrings or hoops to eliminate the risk of their getting stuck on something and tearing an earlobe.

SHOES FOR MUSICAL THEATRE DANCE

Musical theatre dancers use different types of shoes depending on the form of dance used in a particular show. Your instructor will tell you what type of shoe is preferred for class. Some may require ballet shoes, whereas others may suggest jazz sneakers, jazz oxfords, or character shoes.

Ballet Shoes

Ballet shoes are flat slippers made of either leather or canvas that are form fitting and have a thin flexible sole. They have an adjustable drawstring that fits the shoe to the foot and an elastic strap that lies across the arch of the foot to keep the shoe on. Ballet shoes come in pink, white, black, and tan colors.

Character shoes (left), ballet shoes (middle), and jazz oxfords (right).

Jazz Sneakers

Jazz sneakers are thick-soled sneakers that provide shock absorption during jumps but are flexible enough to allow movement. They are often worn for hip-hop choreography. They come in a variety of colors.

Jazz Oxfords

Jazz oxfords are made of leather and are available in a slip-on variety or a lace-up type. They are form fitting and have rubber soles that provide traction when dancing. Some have split soles to allow extra flexibility when using the foot. Some have a slightly raised heel for better shock absorption. They are made in black and tan.

Character Shoes

Character shoes have a raised heel that can range anywhere from 1/2 to 3 inches (1 to 8 cm) high. They have either a buckle strap that runs across the arch of the foot or a T-shaped strap. They are available in black or tan.

FOOT CARE AND PERSONAL HYGIENE

Foot care and personal hygiene are important for all dancers. Because you will always be depending on your feet, you will need to know how to care for them, and because dance is an intense form of physical activity, you will want to pay careful attention to your personal hygiene habits.

Feet

As a dancer, you will be relying on your feet and must therefore give them careful attention. Blisters often form and must be given immediate attention. Antibacterial ointments can help prevent infections, and first-aid tape can help with minor cuts and tears.

When your feet are sore, you can soak them in warm water and Epsom salt baths. Using small rollers and lotions can also help.

You should trim your toenails enough to avoid scratching your legs but leave them long enough to avoid ingrown toenails that can be painful.

Personal Hygiene

Like any type of physical activity, dance causes participants to perspire, and you must pay careful attention to personal hygiene. Showering after every class and washing practice clothes are important habits to develop.

You should wear deodorant to every class out of respect for your fellow dancers and your teacher. Those who are concerned about chemicals present in traditional antiperspirants will find that many natural options are available. Buying inexpensive shoe deodorizers to place in your dance shoes can keep odors from developing in them.

CARRYING DANCE GEAR

A dance bag is a convenient way to carry practice clothes and shoes to and from class. Some other items to consider keeping in your dance bag are antibacterial ointment, first-aid tape, nail clippers, a brush, hair clips, hair elastics, a towel, deodorant, and a journal with a pen or pencil for taking notes or writing down corrections and combinations.

Your dance clothes and shoes will probably be damp with perspiration after class, so you should remove them from your bag to let them air dry. Dance clothes and shoes left in dance bags will develop an odor that will be difficult to get out of the bag. Also, some dance shoes will stretch out when damp and will tend to wear out more quickly than when they have a chance to dry out between classes.

PREPARING YOURSELF PHYSICALLY AND MENTALLY

Dance is a demanding activity that places stress on the body and requires considerable focus and concentration. To prepare yourself both physically and mentally, you should arrive early to class. Dancers are normally expected to arrive at least 10 minutes before a class is scheduled to begin. You should use those 10 minutes to prepare your body and mind for the class.

Physical Preparation

Dance requires the body to move in different ways than it does during normal daily activities. For your muscles to respond to the demands that will be placed on them during class, you need to give your body time to prepare itself. Large, gross-motor, cardiovascular movements such as slow jogging or prancing in place, leg swings, and arm circles will start to warm up your joints and get your blood circulating quicker through your body. Your joints all contain a substance called synovial fluid. At rest that fluid is jelly-like, but as the joints warm up, the jelly turns into a liquid that lubricates your joints to keep them moving smoothly. As the blood flow to your muscles increases, more oxygen and nutrients can be delivered to them to prepare them for the demands you will soon place on them.

You can profitably use the time before class begins if you have had a previous injury. Taking some time to warm up the affected area of the body with some range-of-motion exercises can help decrease your chances of reinjury.

ACTIVITY

PERSONAL WARM-UP

Take time to get to know your body. Lie down, close your eyes, and try to sense where you carry tension or which of your muscles and joints seem to be stiffer than others. Using that awareness, create a short, personal gross-motor warm-up with movements that focus on those areas of your body to do every day before class begins.

Warming up is an important part of preparing your body for dance.

Mental Preparation

You should also use the time before class to get into "the zone." The world inside the dance studio or on the stage is a place where you will need to focus and not allow anything to distract you. Leave conflicts, emotions, and cellphones at the door. You should instead be looking over notes from the previous class, reviewing past combinations, and preparing your mind to learn new material.

Coming to class and performing the exercises and combinations is not enough. You need to spend time outside class reviewing material, repeating the material, evaluating your progress, and working on your presentation and performance skills.

Reviewing Material

Between classes you should think about what was covered in the studio. Review exercises and new steps as well as corrections that have been given to you or to the class as a whole. When a student returns to class and makes the same mistakes that she or he made before, the teacher must repeat the corrections and cannot move forward until they are implemented. Not reviewing before class can impede your progress and the progress of the entire class. This situation becomes frustrating for everyone involved.

Repetition

Repeating and practicing dance phrases and combinations between classes and rehearsals will help you develop **muscle memory**. When you do a movement the first time, a new pathway is formed between the muscles that you use and your brain. Each time you perform the movement, it becomes easier because the pathway has become better developed and more familiar. After you do a movement several times, it becomes automatic, and you do not have to think about it as much.

Repeating phrases will also help you find patterns in the movement that will help you learn new phrases quicker. Besides doing physical repetition, you will benefit by reviewing dance phrases and combinations mentally because doing so will help reinforce the established motor pathways.

Evaluation

Evaluating your personal progress in class will help you stay focused on both your short-term and long-term goals in musical theatre dance. If you get into the habit of thinking about how you performed in class each day, you will be able to see how much progress you are making, determine what you need to work on, and get the most out of the experience.

Presentation and Performance Skills

Even the most experienced dancer will have difficulty learning a dance phrase or combination and immediately performing it well. Learning a sequence is challenging and requires great focus and concentration. After you have learned the sequence, you will need to think about how you are performing it. Although all dancers need to think about their presentation skills, musical theatre dancers must be concerned about the message or mood that the dance phrase is trying to convey and how their individual characters might perform the movements. By working on sequences outside class, you will be prepared to focus on how you dance and be able to perform the phrase the next time you have class.

SUMMARY

To get the most out of a musical theatre dance class, you must show up prepared. By taking the time to dress appropriately and care for yourself, you will be creating a healthy and happy learning environment for everyone. By taking responsibility for yourself, you will allow the teacher to focus on teaching dance and not having to issue reminders about dress codes. By simply arriving to class a few minutes early and preparing yourself both physically and mentally, you will help ensure that the class starts on time and progresses quickly, allowing you to learn as much as possible about musical theatre dance.

To find supplementary materials for this chapter, such as learning activities, e-journal assignments, and web links, visit the web resource at **www.HumanKinetics.com/BeginningMusicalTheatreDance.**

Chapter 3

Safety and Health

Musicians learn how to care for their instruments before they play their first notes. In the same way, dancers need to learn about their instruments: their bodies. Dancers need to have a strong understanding of how the body works, how to care for it, how to protect it from injury, and how to keep it healthy. Dancers also need to understand how to dance safely in the studio and with other dancers.

STUDIO SAFETY

The dance studio must be a safe place for students to move and learn. Some general rules govern how studio space is used to ensure the safety of everyone who dances in the space.

Equipment and Storage

Many dance studios have equipment for use in classes, such as portable or stationary ballet barres, bands for resistance work, weights, fitness or yoga mats, props, and sound systems. This equipment should never be used without supervision or proper instruction.

No food or drink should ever be carried into the studio. Accidental spills or pieces of food could ruin the floor, unnecessarily dirty the studio, and make dancing unsafe. Some studios and teachers allow water bottles in class. Your teacher will let you know whether you can bring water bottles into the studio. Chewing gum is never allowed in a dance studio. Aside from being a choking hazard, gum that falls on the floor becomes a safety issue for others who dance in the space.

Personal belongings such as backpacks, dance bags, phones, and street clothes should be stored securely. Some schools may have a locker room that can be used for storage, but some may not. If no storage area is available, the teacher will designate a place within the studio where you can keep your personal items. All items must be stored in that area; personal items must not be left somewhere in the studio where they can become a hazard for dancers who might trip over them or slip on them. In addition, you must turn off your cell phone so that it does not create a disturbance during class.

PERSONAL SAFETY

Although the rules for the dance studio help ensure that you remain safe in class, you need to think about a few other things. You need to be sure that you dance in your own personal space and do not endanger others. You also need to establish an open line of communication with your teacher about your personal health.

Personal Space

Understanding the concept of **personal space** is important for the safety of both you and your fellow dancers. You should be sure that you have enough space around you to accommodate leg, arm, and body extensions without encroaching on the personal space of another dancer. You need to be aware of where you are in space at all times, whether you are standing in the center, traveling across the floor, or performing a dance.

Personal Health Information

Personal health information is just that—personal information. If you have had an injury or surgery or have a chronic health condition that might affect your physical performance or the health of your peers, you are not obligated to tell everyone, but

Dancers spread out across the studio, establishing personal space.

you should tell your instructor. To protect privacy, instructors usually encourage students to see them after the first class. Your instructor should be aware of any chronic condition or disease such as asthma, diabetes, or epilepsy so that he or she is prepared for a possible emergency and can help you dance safely. An instructor who is not aware of your specific health conditions will be unable to accommodate your needs.

BASIC ANATOMY

The body is made up of various systems that work together to make movement possible. The skeletal system provides the framework for the muscles, and the muscular system is composed of several types of fibers that work together to make movement happen.

Skeletal System

Bones are the foundation of the body (see figure 3.1). When they are aligned correctly, muscles, tendons, and ligaments can do their jobs effectively and efficiently. Bones and joints are designed to provide support and offer shock absorption when dancers run, jump, or leap. But bones can provide this support only if they are in the correct positions. Proper alignment helps prevent injuries and reduces the physical stress that dance places on the body.

When the body is perfectly aligned, muscles are able to move the bones properly, and joints are able to move in the manner they are designed to move. The skeleton should be aligned over the feet, the knees should be directly above the ankles, and the hips should be directly over the knees. The ribcage should be in line with the pelvis and remain neutral, not splayed open or collapsed inward. The pelvis should also be held in a neutral position. If the pelvis is tucked under or swayed back, the natural curves of the spine will be altered. The spinal curves are designed to absorb shock and bend accordingly. The shoulders, neck, and head should be relaxed and sit on top of everything else.

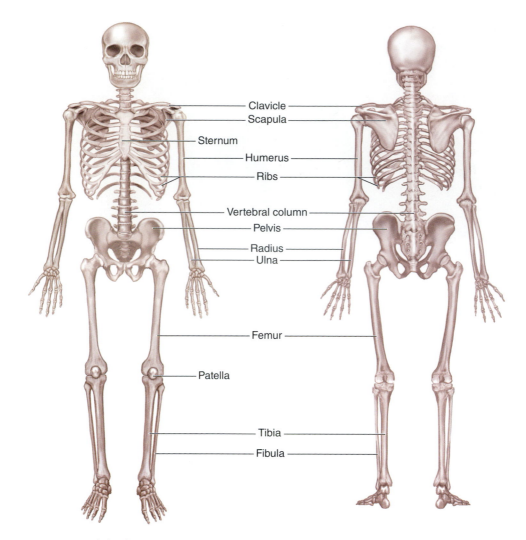

Figure 3.1 Skeletal system.

The focus in dance should always be on lengthening the body, not holding the body in certain positions. If the body is aligned correctly (see figure 3.2), movement will be easier and take less effort, and physical stress will be reduced.

When you are dancing, no matter what position your dancing takes you into, you need to be aware of how your bones are positioned so that you can dance safely and efficiently. For example, good spinal alignment when you are dancing means that your shoulders will be lined up over your hips, usually with the ribs gently hanging in between. Similarly, for leg alignment, your knees will be lined up with the center of your feet as you jump and travel through space.

Alignment is important not only for your bones but also for your muscles. When your skeleton is well aligned, your muscles can work at peak efficiency for the longest duration and with the least risk of injury. The body is a closed system. If you have misaligned the bones in one part of the body, then another part of the body must compensate for that misalignment, leading to an unnecessary expenditure of muscle energy that will tire you quickly. Worse yet, misalignment can be a recipe for injury. Proper alignment is a principle of all forms and styles of dance.

Joints

The place where two bones meet is a joint, and skeletal movement can occur only at joints. The body has five types of joints:

1. Immovable joints—These joints are where two bones meet but no movement occurs. The bones that form these joints offer protection. The bones that make up the skull meet at immovable joints.

2. Ball-and-socket joints—These joints allow movement in all directions. Body parts can flex, or bend; rotate; move toward the body, or adduct; move away from the body, or abduct; and move in a circular motion, or circumduct. This joint is formed where the head of one bone is seated into a hollow spot, or socket, in another bone. The hip joints and shoulder joints are ball-and-socket joints.

Figure 3.2 Proper alignment.

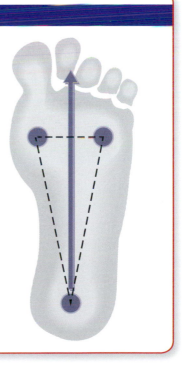

TECHNIQUE TIP

When standing, you should envision a triangle on the bottom of your foot that has one point under the big toe, one point under the smallest toe, and one point under the heel. Body weight should be evenly distributed among those points so that the foot provides a solid foundation. Body weight should not be too far forward or too far backward, and the foot should not be allowed to roll inward or outward. Most students have difficulty learning how to stand correctly. You should work closely with your instructor to remedy any issues you might have in this area to avoid alignment issues and injuries.

3. Hinge joints—These joints allow back and forth movement. Among the many hinge joints in the body are the knees, the elbows, one of the two joints found at the ankle, and the knuckles.

4. Gliding joints—These joints are found in the wrist, the ankle, and the bones of the back, or the vertebrae. They allow sideways movement as one bone slides over the surface of another.

5. Pivot joints—These joints allow twisting up to 180 degrees and are found where the skull and the neck meet and where the pelvis meets the spine.

Muscles, Tendons, and Ligaments

Muscles, tendons, and ligaments are the soft, connective tissues surrounding the skeletal joints that receive information from the brain and react to make movement possible (see figure 3.3).

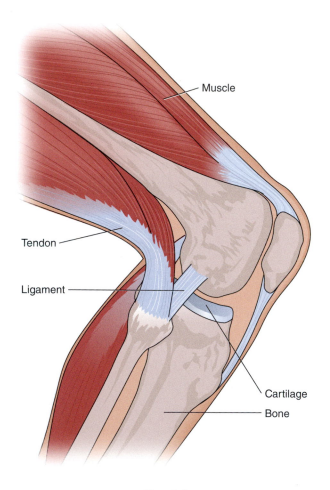

Knee joint

Figure 3.3 Connective tissues.

Muscles

Muscles are composed of thousands of individual fibers. Muscles have four specific properties: excitability, contractility, extensibility, and elasticity.

Excitability means that muscles can receive a message, or stimulus, from the brain and respond to it. Every movement of a dancer is the result of a message traveling from the brain to specific muscle fibers and exciting, or forcing, them to move. The actual movement occurs because of **contractility**. When muscle fibers contract, or shorten, they pull on bones and cause the bones to move. When the movement is completed, **extensibility** allows the muscles to release and return to their extended states. **Elasticity** is an important property because it ensures that no matter how far a muscle is stretched, it will return to its original state.

Dancers should understand that muscles operate in pairs. The muscles that contract to make a movement occur are aided by the opposing muscle group, which lengthens to allow the movement to occur. When the movement is completed and the body needs to return to its original position, the muscles that lengthened to allow the movement must contract and the muscles that previously contracted must lengthen.

Tendons

Tendons are also fibrous tissues. Tendons are responsible for connecting muscles to bones. Additionally, they act as shock absorbers. When a dancer lands from a jump, the tendons absorb some of the impact and distribute the rest of the energy through the muscles. Because tendons can absorb some of this energy, they are also capable of acting as springs and releasing the stored energy the next time a dancer jumps. Like muscles, tendons can be stretched because they are elastic and capable of returning to their original state.

Ligaments

Ligaments have two important jobs. They connect bones to each other, and they limit and prevent movement from occurring. The body operates best when the skeletal bones are perfectly aligned. Ligaments help with alignment by preventing bones from sliding out of place or moving in strange directions. Therefore, ligaments must be tight to do their jobs effectively. Note that ligaments, unlike muscles and tendons, are not elastic, so if they become stretched out they will not be able to return to their original state. A stretched ligament is incapable of holding bones together or limiting movement the way it used to, so the associated joint becomes unstable.

PREVENTING INJURIES

The best ways to prevent injuries are to be knowledgeable about your body and the way it works and to learn about the most common causes of injury in the dance studio. Everyone's body is different. You need to be aware of how your body is feeling and learn to listen to it so that you can approach class in a way that is healthy for you.

Although the teacher will structure the class in a safe manner to ensure that you learn new things gradually, many of the movements will be new to you. Even if you have danced before or participated in sports, you will find that some forms of dance you will be learning will place new and different demands on your body. You need to be patient and have realistic expectations for yourself. Having high goals is admirable, but give yourself permission to learn and master new things slowly and in a way that is healthy for you.

If you ever feel any type of pain, you should let your teacher know. You could be doing an exercise incorrectly and need assistance. You could also have some muscle tightness or body alignment issues. Your teacher may be able to offer some advice and provide supplemental exercises that will help. If you feel you have injured yourself during class, let your teacher know right away. Never try to dance through pain because you could injure yourself even more.

If you have any type of an injury or are not feeling well, tell the teacher before class begins. She or he may suggest that you sit and watch, or you both may decide that you should try to dance and then decide whether you can continue. By letting the teacher know at the beginning of class, she or he will understand if you need to leave the dance floor or studio.

Each school and each teacher will have policies about class absences. If you are contagious, running a fever, or experiencing stomach issues, staying at home would probably be best. But if you are simply not feeling well enough to dance, watching class would be beneficial. You will be able to take notes on what is covered in class that day so that you do not miss anything.

Environmental Factors

The type of floor, stage, or dancing surface is always a concern for dancers. Because dancers are constantly jumping, leaping, and performing falls to the floor, the surface should be able to absorb shock so that the body does not absorb all the impact. Wooden floors can help absorb shock. Wooden, sprung floors are the best surface choice because the pockets of air trapped underneath this type of floor help absorb impact energy.

DID YOU KNOW?

Many dance groups use portable vinyl floors that can be laid over any type of surface. These floors provide optimal traction for dancers.

Concrete floors provide no energy absorption. Dancers who perform on concrete floors place tremendous strain on their bodies and often suffer from chronic injuries like shin splints, stress fractures, and tendinitis.

Slippery floors are also a concern for dancers. They are dangerous because dancers must depend on the dancing surface to provide traction when they are moving, jumping, and turning. A substance called rosin can be used on dance shoes to help provide traction if a floor is extremely slippery. Dancers, however, need to be careful not to use too much rosin because it can cause the feet to get stuck in spots on the floor, which can cause other problems.

Internal Factors

Although the environment is a significant consideration in causes of injury in dance, some internal factors related to the body can predispose you to injury. Some of these factors are failure to warm up and cool down, poor technique, fatigue, and muscular imbalances.

You must always warm up before each class. A warm-up that contains gross-motor movements that use large muscles increases the heart rate, which increases blood flow and ensures that necessary oxygen and nutrients are delivered to the muscles. A warm-up also increases body temperature. When muscle temperature increases, muscle fibers become more flexible. A warm-up also helps liquefy the synovial fluid found in the joints. When the fluid is cold, it is jelly-like, but as heat is generated, it becomes a liquid that lubricates the joints and keeps them moving smoothly.

Cooling down after class is also important. During a cool-down the heart rate and breathing rate return to normal. Stretching during a cool-down helps eliminate muscle cramping when you leave the studio.

Technique classes teach dancers how to execute exercises properly. During these classes, teachers check for proper alignment and make sure that the dancers are using the correct muscles. When the dancers' bodies are not properly aligned, their bodies cannot move efficiently and joints will be unstable and compromised.

Physical and mental fatigue can also cause injuries. When dancers have been spending long hours in classes or rehearsals, their bodies grow tired. Messages between the brain and muscles are not processed as quickly and efficiently in a fatigued body as they would be in a well-rested one. When this communication slows down or begins to break down, the muscles cannot respond quickly and properly, so injuries can occur.

Dancers stretch after class to cool down and increase flexibility.

Muscular imbalances are another problem for dancers. Because dancers are always using the same groups of muscles, these muscles tend to be stronger and tighter than other muscles. Because muscle groups work in pairs, if one group is tighter than its opposing group, the tighter muscles will pull on the skeleton unevenly and pull it out of alignment, causing joint instability that can lead to injuries.

TREATING COMMON DANCE INJURIES

All injuries should be cared for using the **PRICED method**—protection, rest, ice, compression, elevation, and diagnosis. As soon as the dancer experiences an injury, the injured body part should be protected by moving off the dance floor. Resting the injury will allow it time to heal.

When an injury occurs, the body's natural response is to flood the injured area with substances called macrophages and proteins. Macrophages, the body's "garbage men," are sent in to remove damaged cells and tissue. **Proteins** are necessary to begin repairs. Unfortunately, the body does not know when to stop flooding the injured area, so swelling occurs.

Ice, compression, and elevation help limit the amount of substances directed toward the injured area. Ice helps constrict the capillaries, or blood vessels, that supply the substances. Ice should be applied for 20 minutes several times a day for the first 48 to 72 hours following an injury. Compression prevents more fluid from entering the area, and elevating the injured part above the heart makes it difficult for the body to continue to pump fluid to it.

SAFETY TIP

Apply ice to an injured area in 20-minute intervals to prevent frostbite from occurring. After 72 hours, heat can be applied to help encourage healing. A sports medicine or dance medicine specialist should diagnose all injuries to determine severity.

TRAINING VERSUS FITNESS

Dancers need to understand the difference between dance training and fitness. Dance training helps increase bone density and develops muscular strength, muscular endurance, and flexibility specifically as they pertain to dance. Fitness focuses on the entire body.

Cross-training in various sports can help dancers develop cardiorespiratory fitness, muscular strength and endurance, and flexibility equally throughout the entire body.

Cardiorespiratory Fitness

Cardiorespiratory fitness is a major concern for dancers. This aspect is measured by how efficiently your heart and lungs work to deliver oxygen to cells in your body. Cardiorespiratory fitness is developed through exercises of low intensity and long duration. During most dance classes, movement frequently stops and starts many times. Dancers must pause to learn a step, sequence, or combination and then dance it. This type of activity does not build stamina and is not effective at building cardiorespiratory fitness. This type of fitness will be of extreme concern for you as a musical theatre dancer because you must use oxygen to sustain singing as well as movement. Walking, running, swimming, and biking are all activities that can help you develop cardiorespiratory fitness.

Bone Density

Bone density, a measure of the amount of minerals in a given area of bone, is an indicator of bone strength. Bone responds to pressure. Each time an external force places stress on the bones, the body responds by adding another layer of minerals to protect itself. Each time we run, walk, jump, or use weights, we are encouraging our bodies to strengthen our skeletons. Dance is an activity that is effective at increasing bone density. Increased bone density helps protect against osteoporosis, a disease characterized by weakened bones that become brittle and break easily.

Muscular Strength and Endurance

Muscular strength is the maximum amount of force that a muscle or muscle group can exert, whereas **muscular endurance** is the ability of a muscle or muscle group to contract repeatedly over time. Dance helps develop both muscular strength and endurance. Exercises in dance are designed to strengthen and develop muscles and tendons so that they will be capable of performing dance steps and combinations. The long hours spent in class and rehearsal require continual muscle use, which helps develop muscular endurance. Dancers need to be aware, however, that although dance develops certain muscles groups, it may not strengthen all muscles evenly throughout the body, so muscular imbalances occur. Tighter muscles can pull unevenly on the skeleton and create problems at joints, causing the skeleton to be pulled out of proper alignment. Cross-training with Pilates, yoga, or strength and conditioning classes can help ensure that all muscles are developed and help keep imbalances from occurring.

Flexibility

Flexibility measures the range of motion that occurs at a joint. Dancers need to be able to move in many ways with ease. Muscles that are too tight will limit your range of motion and are prone to injury. Both **dynamic stretching** and **static stretching** can help increase your flexibility and enhance your dancing. Dynamic stretching is active stretching during which the body is constantly moving. Many dance exercises include a dynamic stretch. This type of stretching works range of motion and increases muscular strength. It can be done at any time. Static stretching is passive. These types of stretches are held for 20 to 30 seconds. Although they are effective at increasing range of motion, they should be done only at the end of class or rehearsal because they can temporarily decrease muscular strength and power.

NUTRITION, HYDRATION, AND REST

In addition to properly training, dancers must be sure to care for their bodies correctly. Food is the fuel for the body. Learning about how the body uses food to create energy and making healthy choices about what to eat before, during, and after classes and rehearsals can improve your performance. Knowing how to keep the body properly hydrated and understanding the role that rest plays in exercise recovery will help you be a healthy dancer.

Nutrition

The body needs fuel, which comes in the form of food. Eating healthy and at the proper times will help ensure that you have the necessary energy for class, rehearsals, and performance. Eating several small meals a day will help increase your **metabolism**, the speed at which your body is able to convert food into energy.

The body's primary source for energy is carbohydrate, which should make up about 60 percent of your diet. The two categories of carbohydrate are simple carbohydrate and complex carbohydrate. Your body easily digests simple carbohydrates found in food like white bread, white rice, and sugar and converts them to energy immediately. As a result, you will experience a tremendous burst of energy that disappears quickly. Complex carbohydrate is digested slowly. The body needs more time to metabolize food that contains complex carbohydrates. Because the process is gradual, complex carbohydrate can be compared to a timed-release supplement. The energy is created over a longer time, lasts longer, and dissipates gradually. Consuming complex carbohydrates several hours before a class or a performance will provide you with the necessary energy to perform well and feel your best. Some food made up of complex carbohydrates that you might consider adding to your diet are whole-grain breads and pastas, whole-grain crackers, brown rice, quinoa, oats, and pretzels.

> ## DID YOU KNOW?
>
> Not all wheat breads are healthy choices. Be sure to check the ingredient list for "whole-wheat flour." If a label lists "enriched wheat flour" as an ingredient, some of the nutritional value has been removed from the grain.

The body's secondary energy source is fat. Although the body uses carbohydrate first, after about 20 minutes of exercise, it begins to rely on stored fat for fuel. Healthy fat should make up about 25 percent of your diet. Healthy fats are monounsaturated fat and polyunsaturated fat. Besides providing energy, fat also strengthens your immune system and acts as a building block for hormones. Trans fat should be avoided because it is difficult for the body to digest and it contributes to heart disease by clogging arteries and creating blockages. Avoiding foods high in trans fat like chips, processed foods, doughnuts, and fried foods and choosing foods like olive oil, nut butters, nuts, olives, and avocados will keep you healthier.

Protein should account for about 15 percent of your diet. The body uses protein to repair damaged tissues and maintain muscular health. Protein also supplies the body with minerals like zinc, iron, and niacin. A high-protein meal or snack is the perfect choice after a class, rehearsal, or performance. Good sources of protein are meats, fish, soy, dairy products, and eggs.

Hydration

For your body to work well, it must be properly hydrated. Drinking water before, during, and after class or rehearsal will keep your body working efficiently and replace fluids that you lose in sweat as you dance.

Water is the best choice for hydration. The carbonation in soft drinks will make you feel full before you are adequately hydrated. Juices are high in sugar and can cause cramping during exercise, and sports drinks contain dyes and corn syrup, which are not healthy choices.

Rest

Rest is essential for everyone, especially dancers. You should try to get a full eight hours of sleep each night. Sleep may not seem important, but while you are sleeping, a lot is going on that can make your next day productive. The body is able to spend time repairing itself while you sleep. Your body is your instrument in dance, and because you use your body in your daily life, the only real break it gets is when you sleep. Muscles have a chance to relax and repair, and your brain has the opportunity to regroup. When you sleep, the brain consolidates all the information that it gathers during the day. A good night's sleep will lead to better physical performance, better ability to concentrate and focus, and greater ability to remember and perform combinations and dances.

SUMMARY

By learning about your body, you can become familiar with your instrument, dance safely and efficiently, and dance for your entire life. Knowing how to avoid injuries and caring for injuries when they occur will ensure that you remain healthy. Cross-training to promote fitness will help you become a stronger dancer, and eating, drinking, and resting properly will keep you performing happily and at peak levels.

To find supplementary materials for this chapter, such as learning activities, e-journal assignments, and web links, visit the web resource at **www.HumanKinetics.com/BeginningMusicalTheatreDance.**

WEB RESOURCE

Chapter 4

Learning and Performing Musical Theatre Dance

In many ways, entering a dance studio is like traveling to a foreign country. The experience can be an adventure, but you will need to learn the languages of dance and theatre, develop the skills required for learning movement, and understand the relationship between dance and music. Dance training is challenging because of the demands placed on the body as well as the mind. You may need several classes to begin to feel comfortable in the studio.

Although you will likely be studying a variety of dance forms as your class progresses, some guidelines can help you learn any type of movement. Learning movement vocabulary, discovering ways to learn and memorize movement quickly, and developing your sense of musicality will help you as you begin this adventure.

LANGUAGE OF MUSICAL THEATRE DANCE

The vocabulary used in musical theatre dance ranges from general, descriptive terms that can be applied to any type of movement to the names of specific steps within a particular dance form.

Movement and Choreographic Vocabulary

Movement and choreographic terms can be applied to all forms of dance and all combinations of movement, from gestural movements to well-established and developed dance phrases. They define where and how the movement takes place and is performed.

Space

The concepts of positive and negative space play a big role in how musical theatre dancers communicate with the audience. **Positive space** is the space filled by the body, and **negative space** is the empty space between body parts, dancers, or actors. When used effectively, positive and negative space can have a huge effect on how a story is told onstage. The use of space is imperative in a scene like the dream ballet from *Carousel*. During the musical, the main character, Billy Bigelow, is killed and allowed to return to Earth for one day to see his teenage daughter whom he has never met. The distance and space between the two characters throughout the scene serves to build tension as they gesture toward each other but never quite connect until they come together for one brief moment at the end.

Positive and negative space is also used effectively in the song "America" from *West Side Story*. An argument ensues as the females and males discuss the pros and cons of being Puerto Rican and living in America. As the females move toward the males, the males back away, and as the males encroach upon the females, they, too, back away, creating a push and pull that is an image of the verbal argument.

Levels

The use of levels in dances keeps the movement alive and interesting to watch. Some dancers may perform movements on a low level, while others simultaneously perform movements at a middle level, and still others perform on a high level. Generally, the **low level** is defined as the space close to the floor, the **middle level** is the space we move in on a daily basis, and the **high level** is the space over our heads that we occupy when we jump or stand on our toes.

This movement tool allows everyone to be seen and creates an interesting visual for the audience. The use of multiple levels is especially effective in held positions at the beginning or end of phrases or when one group of dancers moves from a low position through a middle position to a high position while another group simultaneously moves from a high position through a middle position to a low position.

Choreographers use low, middle, and high levels to create interesting poses.

Directions and Pathways

Rarely does movement stay in one place for long. You will be asked to learn movement phrases and perform them while traveling from one point to another.

Dancers are often taught a phrase that moves across the space sideways from left to right and begins on the right foot. After learning the phrase, you will be expected to reverse that phrase, starting on the left foot and traveling in the opposite direction. Some phrases also move forward and backward to add variety to the choreography.

The use of various **pathways** on the stage also adds variety to the choreography. Although straight lines can be used, movement that travels on a diagonal line can signify the passage of time. The use of shapes like diamonds, V shapes, X shapes, and circles adds yet another level of interest. A circle is often the traditional pathway of movement in folk or social dance forms.

Focus

Another important part of movement is learning about **focus** and how much it adds to a dance phrase.

You need to be aware of where you are focusing, or looking, while you dance. Focus can be used to create a picture of unity while dancing, and it provides a neat and clean appearance to the audience. It can also be used to direct an audience's attention to a particular part of the stage to move the plot line along.

Unison Movement

Unison movement describes dances in which everyone performs the same movements, in the same manner, at the same time. Unison dancing can make a powerful statement. In unison dancing, everyone must dance in the same way; legs, arms, hands, and heads must move in the same direction at the same time.

The final scene from *A Chorus Line* features a unison dance to the song "One." The dancers are costumed identically in gold costumes and top hats, and they perform precise, identical movements including chorus line kicks. The unison movement creates a spectacular sight for the audience and emphasizes the show's main idea that all Broadway performers long for the same goals in spite of differing backgrounds and experiences.

Fans and Ripples

Fans, or ripples, are simple gestures that occur in a successive pattern. The gesture is performed by one dancer and then immediately performed in turn by the succeeding dancers until everyone has completed it. Fans are similar to "the wave" that is performed in sport arenas.

Canons

A **canon** is a choreographic technique used to make dances more interesting to watch. In canons, every dancer performs the same movement phrase at different times. The dancers are divided into groups, and each group begins the phrase at a designated time in the music. The following is an example of a canon:

Group A begins the phrase right away.

Group B waits to begin until 8 counts after group A begins.

Group C waits to begin the phrase until 16 counts after group A begins.

Specific Dance Vocabulary

Often, vocabulary used in your dance class will be specific to particular dance forms. Each step has a unique name. As class progresses, you will learn the names of steps by associating them with the specific movements they define. Writing the names in a journal or notebook will help you become familiar with this vocabulary.

Table 4.1 shows examples of exercises and steps common to most dance forms, but you will also need to know the names of some ballet, jazz, folk, and social dance steps because musical theatre dance borrows from all those forms.

Table 4.1   Some Exercises and Steps in Musical Theatre Dance

	Common	Ballet	Jazz	Social dance	Folk dance
Exercises	Plié Elevé Relevé Forced arch Flick Tendu Dégagé Développé Grand battement	Port de bras	Jazz hands Isolations Contractions Flat back Tilt Splits Jazz splits Lunges	Basic partner positions	
Steps	Chassé Pas de bourrée Grapevine Ball change	Ballet walks Bourrée Tombé Balancé Waltz step	Fan kicks Jazz walks Jazz runs Jazz square	Step hop Triple step Rock step Box step	Step Stomp Heel and toe Do si do Polka Schottische
Turns	Three-step turn Pirouette Chaînés Soutenu turn	Pique	Pivot turns		
Jumps	Sauté Leap	Jeté Pas de chat Arabesque sauté	Hitch kick Stag leap Tuck jump		

Theatre Terminology

Besides learning dance vocabulary, you will need to learn the language of the theatre. Knowing about the types of stages and the terminology used to refer to parts of the stage will ease your transition from the studio to the theatre.

Types of Stages

Not all theatres are the same. Although they all likely have a stage, a seating area, and a lobby, the layout can vary significantly. You should know the differences between proscenium arch stages, thrust stages, and arena stages.

In a **proscenium arch theatre**, an arch frames the stage and separates the stage from the audience section of the theatre (see figure 4.1). The stage is raised, and all of the audience seating faces the front of the stage. The theatre may have balconies for additional seating and an orchestra pit between the stage and the audience for live musicians.

In a **thrust stage theatre**, the stage extends out into the audience section of the theatre. The audience is seated around the three sides of the raised platform that extends the stage forward. This type of stage brings the performers closer to the audience but requires the performers to project in three directions instead of one.

An **arena stage** is an open space on the floor in the middle of the auditorium. The audience is seated around the space in raised, bleacher-type seating, and the performers must perform **in the round**. Performing in the round means that the performers are seen from all directions, and they will be constantly projecting to the audience.

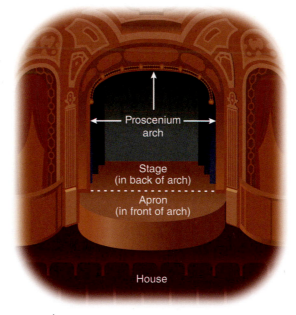

Figure 4.1 Proscenium arch stage.

Stage Directions

Stage directions are labels, usually abbreviated, given to different areas of the stage. They help everyone working on a show determine where scenery might be, where action might be happening, and what space can be used. The stage is divided into a grid with 15 squares (see figure 4.2).

The directions **stage right** and **stage left** are based on the performer's perspective when the performer is facing the audience and standing in the center of the stage. The area to the performer's right is considered stage right, and the area to the performer's left is considered stage left.

The following abbreviations and grid will help you learn the parts of the stage:

U = upstage

D = downstage

R = stage right

L = stage left

C = center stage

These abbreviations can be combined to indicate areas like upstage center, UC, or downstage to the left of center, DLC.

The more time you spend studying musical theatre dance, the more familiar you will become with this vocabulary and terminology. As you learn dances, you will begin to associate the vocabulary and terminology with movements, and everything will seem less foreign.

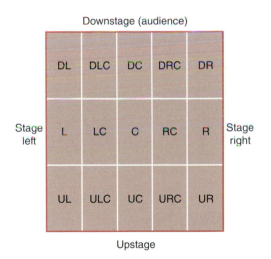

Figure 4.2 Stage diagram.

LEARNING DANCE STEPS, PHRASES, AND DANCES

Being aware of how your body processes new information will help you learn in class and help you to be patient with yourself. The human brain has to move through three steps to create a memory. First, the brain must gather information from the senses, which dancers do visually, auditorily, and kinesthetically. Second, the brain organizes the information. Third, through repetition, the information is committed to memory.

Because new movements and phrases are usually demonstrated three times in class, focusing on one sensory piece at a time makes sense. Trying to absorb too much input at once will overload your brain and hinder your learning.

Visual Learning

Visual learning refers to how we learn when we gather information through our sense of sight. The first time a new movement is demonstrated, you need to watch it carefully, to focus intently on what is happening. Your brain receives a lot of information every day. If you do not concentrate on what you are seeing, your brain will treat the demonstration as just another thing going on in your surroundings. Intentionally watching the teacher demonstrate the movements will help you learn them.

Auditory Learning

Auditory learning happens when we use our hearing to gather information. The second time a combination is demonstrated in class, you should begin to try the movement and to focus on listening to what the teacher is saying while moving. Your teacher may say the names of the steps or count out the movement so that you begin to understand how the movement relates to the music.

Kinesthetic Learning

Kinesthetic learning occurs when our bodies actually perform the movements. Information is gathered through sensors in our muscles. By doing the movements, we begin to develop pathways between the working muscles and the brain. These motor pathways are reinforced each time we physically do the movement, watch the movement being performed, or imagine ourselves doing it. After demonstrating the combination twice, your teacher will probably suggest that you **mark** the combination. Marking means going through all the movements to help you learn and memorize them. You should do all the movements but use a bit less energy than you will when your teacher asks you to do an actual performance of the phrase or combination.

> **TECHNIQUE TIP**
>
> When marking an exercise, you can walk through the movements with your feet, but you should always use your arms and head as you would when you will actually be performing the combination.

UNDERSTANDING MUSICALITY

Musicality concerns your knowledge of the music and your sensitivity to it. In almost all genres of dance, movement and music work together to create a relationship that helps convey emotion or meaning. This relationship is especially important in musical theatre dance in which dance and music work together to tell a story. You will need to learn how to dance with the music and relate how you dance to the mood of the music.

Relating Movement to the Music

Knowing basic information about how music is phrased will help you hear the beat of the music, learn to count the music, and learn how to connect your movement to it.

Common time signatures used in music are 4/4 time, 2/4 time, and 3/4 time. In 4/4 time, a measure has 4 beats. In 2/4 time, a measure has 2 beats. Both of these time signatures are common in ballet, jazz, tap, and folk dance.

In 3/4 time, a measure has 3 beats. This time signature is known as waltz time, and it has a swinging feeling to it. The 3/4 time signature is common in music used for ballet, folk dance, and social dancing.

Counting Music

Dancers count dance movements in phrases of eight counts. Each movement may require one count, slower movements may take multiple counts, and quick movements may happen between the counts on the "and" phrase of counting: 1 and 2 and 3 and 4.

UNDERSTANDING ARTISTRY AND ARTISTIC DEVELOPMENT

Artistry can be defined as creative skill or ability, and artistic development occurs when you begin to think about how you are dancing. Movements, gestures, level changes, and pathways mean nothing to an audience if there is no intent behind

---

ACTIVITY

EXPLORE MOVEMENT QUALITIES

To develop an understanding of how different movement qualities can create a different feeling, try doing a simple movement like reaching out toward something. First, in a sustained movement, begin extending your arm toward something in a continuous motion until it is fully extended. Now try reaching out toward something and pulling your arm back in quickly as if your hand has been burned to create a percussive movement quality. Try the same movement using your arm in a swinging, or pendular, quality or while the arm is shaking, or vibrating.

Adding intentional movement qualities and dynamics helps a simple gesture begin to tell a story.

the movement. Although artistic development is important in all dance genres, it is extremely important in musical theatre dance. The movements need to be performed in a manner consistent with the personality of a particular character and in a way that communicates a specific message to the audience. Using various **movement qualities** and **dynamics** in choreography is what makes this communication possible. Movement quality describes how energy is applied to create a motion. A motion in which energy is continuously applied is a sustained movement that is seen as being smooth and continuous, whereas a motion created by energy starting and stopping is considered a percussive movement. Some other movement qualities are swinging, vibratory, suspending, and collapsing. Dynamics refers to the intensity of the energy used. For example, dynamically, a movement can be slow or fast, strong or weak, heavy or light.

APPLYING AESTHETIC PRINCIPLES

Aesthetic principles are the guidelines and standards by which all art is judged. These standards guide dance teachers and choreographers as they teach dance and create dance sequences.

Several general aesthetic principles are important in dance:

Unity—This principle focuses on being certain that all the movements relate to a unifying theme or intention.

Balance—This principle focuses on making certain that all parts of the dance are proportional to each other. It provides a sense of equality.

Variety—This principle focuses on using various movements, steps, pathways, and directions to challenge the dancer and keep the audience interested.

Repetition—This principle focuses on recurring movements throughout the dance. Repetition provides a connection to the audience members instead of a constant bombardment of new sensory input.

Contrast—This principle focuses on highlighting different parts of a dance to emphasize important movements and messages. This principle helps avoid monotony.

These principles all work together to help dancers become artists who can communicate with the audience.

Applying aesthetic principles and developing artistry are not separate skills from dance training. Because dance is a performing art, you begin to develop artistry as soon as you walk into a dance studio for the first time. Each exercise in class should be performed intentionally. Artistry is not something that is saved for the stage. Each time you dance, you must remember that you are an artist delivering a message.

SUMMARY

Learning any form of dance is a challenge. As a musical theatre dance student, you will face a greater challenge because you need to learn about both the field of dance and the field of theatre. Knowing what to expect in dance class and becoming familiar with the vocabulary used in both the dance studio and the theatre will help prepare you for the journey from training to performing.

To find supplementary materials for this chapter, such as learning activities, e-journal assignments, and web links, visit the web resource at **www.HumanKinetics.com/BeginningMusicalTheatreDance.**   **WEB RESOURCE** ▶

Chapter 5

Basics of Musical Theatre Dance Technique

The musical theatre dance class is structured to expose you to a variety of dance forms and their respective styles, as well as standard steps shared by all of them, as you move from the warm-up to the performance section of class. Familiarity with a variety of forms, styles, and dance vocabulary will make it easier for you to audition and get a role performing in a musical. This knowledge will prepare you to execute a variety of choreographic visions.

Although all classes follow a standard format, the tone of the class may change, depending on the form and style of dance being taught on a particular day. Your class will always begin with a warm-up that will be followed by center work, which includes traveling exercises that move across the dance space, and conclude with the learning of a dance combination from a particular musical.

WARM-UP EXERCISES

The first portion of any dance class includes movements designed to raise the core temperature of your body. The warm-up gets your body moving and helps you mentally focus your energy on what is happening in the studio.

Your class will probably start with some type of cardiovascular warm-up like jogging in place, flicks, full-body circles, or other gross-motor movements involving the entire body. After that, the class will progress through a series of pliés, foot exercises like elevés and relevés, tendus, dégagés, développés, grand battements, and body swings.

Besides raising the temperature of your muscles and joints, the warm-up will increase your heart rate and increase your breathing rate so that plenty of oxygen will be available for use by your muscles. Although your teacher may choose to tailor your warm-up to complement whatever dance form is being taught, some positions and exercises are common across many forms and can be considered standard exercises.

ACTIVITY

FIND YOUR NATURAL TURNOUT

Stand with your feet in parallel first, extend your right leg to the front, lift your foot off the floor, rotate your leg outward from the hip, and then slide it back into position under your hip. Do the same with your left leg. You will then be standing in the turned-out first position that is appropriate for your body.

After a brief bout of cardiovascular exercise, the warm-up typically continues with pliés.

FOOT POSITIONS ON THE FLOOR

Dance is based on five basic foot positions, some of which can be executed in either a turned-out position or a parallel position (see figures 5.1 through 5.8). In the turned-out positions, also called ballet positions, your legs are rotated outward from the hips and the inside arches of your feet face the audience. In the parallel positions, also called jazz positions, your toes and knees face forward toward the audience.

Figure 5.1 First position turned out (ballet first): The heels of the feet touch, and the legs are equally rotated.

Figure 5.2 First position parallel (jazz first): The feet are placed side by side, and the knees are facing forward.

Figure 5.3 Second position turned out (ballet second): The feet are separated by about one and a half foot lengths, and the legs are equally rotated outward.

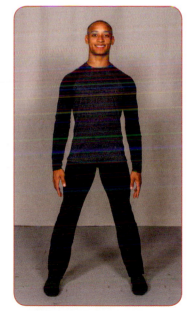

Figure 5.4 Second position parallel (jazz second): The feet are separated by about one and a half foot lengths, and the toes and knees are facing forward.

Figure 5.5 Third position turned out (ballet third): The heel of the front foot touches the middle arch of the back foot, and both legs are outwardly rotated.

Figure 5.6 Fourth position turned out (ballet fourth): The front foot is about one dancer's foot length in front of the back foot, and both legs are outwardly rotated.

Figure 5.7 Fourth position parallel (jazz fourth): The front foot is about one dancer's foot length in front of the back foot, and the knees and toes are facing forward.

Figure 5.8 Fifth position turned out (ballet fifth): The heel of the front foot touches the toe of the back foot, and both legs are outwardly rotated.

Some forms of dance, like ballet, use a **pointed foot** most of the time, whereas other forms, like jazz and modern, use either a pointed foot or a **flexed foot**. In the pointed position (figure 5.9), the foot extends from the ankle as the arch lifts and the toes stretch downward. In the flexed position, the foot bends at the ankle, the arch of the foot is pulled toward the shin, and the toes extend upward (figure 5.10). Both positions can be used touching the floor or in the air.

Figure 5.9   Pointed foot.

Figure 5.10   Flexed foot.

Both full-foot and demi-pointe positions are used in almost all dance forms. In the **full-foot position**, the entire foot is on the floor and the weight is equally distributed between the toes and the heel. In **demi-pointe**, the heel is raised off the floor and the dancer balances on the toes and ball of the foot.

DID YOU KNOW?

Demi-pointe is a ballet term. In French, it means "halfway to the toe."

PORT DE BRAS AND ARM POSITIONS

The literal translation of **port de bras** is "carriage of the arms." In ballet, this term refers to the movements of the arms as they pass through the five basic arm positions (see figures 5.11 through 5.15). The arms are rounded and move from the shoulders in a graceful, fluid manner.

Figure 5.11　First position.

Figure 5.12　Second position.

Figure 5.13　Third position.

Figure 5.14　Fourth position.

Figure 5.15　Fifth position.

LEG AND FOOT POSITIONS IN THE AIR

The legs and feet occupy standard positions when they are lifted into the air. The leg that is lifted off the floor is known as the **working leg**, and the leg on which the dancer balances is referred to as the **supporting leg**.

Coupé—The working leg bends at the knee, and the foot touches the supporting leg at the ankle or middle of the lower leg. A coupé can be placed to the front or back of the supporting leg in a turned-out position or to the side of the ankle or middle of the lower leg in a turned-out or parallel position (figures 5.16 through 5.19).

Figure 5.16   Coupé front.

Figure 5.17   Coupé side turned out.

Figure 5.18   Coupé side parallel.

Figure 5.19   Coupé back.

Retiré—The working leg bends at the knee, and the foot touches the supporting leg at the knee (figures 5.20 through 5.23). Like coupé, the retiré can be placed to the front of the knee in a turned-out position, to the side of the knee in a turned-out or parallel position, or to the back of the supporting knee in a turned-out position.

Figure 5.20   Retiré front.

Figure 5.21   Retiré side turned out.

Figure 5.22   Retiré side parallel.

Figure 5.23   Retiré back.

Arabesque—The body is balanced on the supporting leg, and the working leg extends behind at 45 degrees or higher. This position can be performed in either a parallel (figure 5.24) or turned-out position (figure 5.25). The arabesque can be a pose or part of a step that moves either vertically or horizontally.

Figure 5.24 Arabesque—parallel.

Figure 5.25 Arabesque—turned out.

STATIONARY EXERCISES

Just as some standard positions are used by a variety of dance forms, some stationary exercises are standard. These exercises continue to warm up the body and start to develop your dance technique in each dance form.

Pliés begin to warm up the larger joints of the body, focusing on the hips, knees, and ankles and helping to reinforce proper body alignment.

Demi-plié—Standing in one of the five positions, either turned out or parallel, you bend your knees as far as you can without lifting the heels off the floor and then return to the original stretched position. Be sure that the knees track directly over the toes as they bend.

Grand plié—You execute a demi-plié and continue to descend to a position where the thighs are parallel to the floor. The heels lift only as much as necessary to accommodate this movement. You then return through demi-plié to the original stretched position. The one exception to this rule is that in second position the heels do not release from the floor.

Elevés, relevés, and forced arches are exercises that warm up the feet and lower legs while helping you to learn how to adjust your body to gain your balance.

Elevé—In any position, you simply press down into the floor, lift your heels up off the floor to demi-pointe, and then lower your heels to return to the original position. The entire exercise is performed with straight legs.

Relevé—In any position, execute a demi-plié and as you straighten the legs, press up onto the balls of your feet to demi-pointe. As you lower the heels, bend your knees to return to the demi-plié and then return to a stretched position.

Forced arch—This position can be a held position or one that you move through. It is a rise to demi-pointe with bent knees.

Flick—This exercise helps strengthen the foot and develop foot articulation. Press down into the floor with the working foot until it moves with a flicking motion from a flat-foot position to a pointed position in the air, moving from the ankle. A flick can be used to warm up the muscles and tendons of the foot and lower leg as well as help you understand how to use your foot against the floor and articulate through the various parts of the foot.

Tendus and dégagés continue to warm up your feet and increase foot articulation. They are important exercises because they also begin to work on weight shifting, proper alignment, and technique. For the working leg to perform the exercise, body weight must be transferred to the supporting leg and then transferred back to both feet when the exercise is completed.

Tendu—This exercise warms up the foot and ankle. The working foot slides along the floor, moving away from the body through a demi-pointe to a full pointed position on the floor. As the foot returns, the toes flex first and the foot moves through a demi-pointe position and back to the starting position. Tendus are usually executed from first or fifth position and can be done parallel or turned out. They can be done with straight legs throughout or with a demi-plié upon opening or closing.

Dégagé—This exercise warms up the foot, ankle, and hip. The full foot brushes the floor, moves through a pointe tendu, and ends with the foot about an inch (2.5 cm) off the floor. It then returns to the floor through the tendu position and brushes closed. Dégagés are usually executed from first or fifth position and can be done parallel or turned out. They can be done with straight legs throughout or with a demi-plié upon opening or closing.

Développés and grand battements are exercises that use the entire leg. They should be done only when the body is completely warmed up. They emphasize proper alignment and positioning and focus on developing strength, balance, and control.

Développé—This exercise warms up the leg and hip. The foot moves through coupé to retiré and begins to unfold into a stretched position up to 90 degrees. The leg is then lowered straight and moves through a tendu position back to the original position. Développés normally begin from first or fifth position. They can be executed turned out or parallel and to the front, side, or back.

Grand battement—This exercise is for the leg and hips. The working foot brushes the floor, pointing as it moves through tendu to dégagé, and continues to extend until it reaches at least 90 degrees in the air. The working leg is then lowered through dégagé to tendu to close. Grand battements normally begin from first or fifth position. They can be executed turned out or parallel and to the front, side, or back.

Body circles—This exercise warms up the upper body. Beginning with the body fully extended and the arms reaching straight overhead, you circle your torso first to the right while reaching sideways, then to the floor while reaching down and looking at your legs, and finally to the left while reaching sideways before returning to your original position. You then reverse the movement, starting the circle to the left.

CENTER WORK

After the warm-up, more focused work begins. The teacher will introduce actual steps that will be used in dance phrases and combinations, and you will practice the steps in various patterns and traveling sequences.

Standard Steps

Some standard traveling steps used in a variety of dance forms allow you to move through the space. The footwork remains the same, but the steps can be performed with stylistic differences that reflect the dance forms and styles being used.

Chassé—This sliding step can travel in any direction. One foot "chases" the other. It is executed from a plié in a closed position like first, third, or fifth. The starting foot slides away from the body while staying in full contact with the floor. The chasing foot then slides forward to meet it. Both feet release into the air and point as the legs fully extend before landing in a plié in the original position.

Pas de bourrée—This exercise changes stylistically when performed in different dance forms, but it remains mechanically the same. The step is used to change weight from one foot to the other and can be executed parallel or turned out. This exercise begins and ends with a demi-plié. As you demi-plié, the weight shifts to the supporting leg as the starting foot steps back. The other foot steps to the side, and the original foot then steps forward into a demi-plié. In ballet, it begins and ends in a closed position. In jazz, modern, and tap, it can begin and end in a lunge or almost any position.

Grapevine—This step is called a grapevine because the pattern that the feet make is similar to the twisting nature in which a grapevine grows. The step alternates feet. You begin by stepping out with one foot and then crossing the other foot in front. The original foot steps out again, and the second foot crosses in back. The step pattern alternates as well; the first cross is either in front or behind. This step can be performed repeatedly, so it is frequently used as a traveling step.

Ball change—This step shifts the weight from one foot to the other and back again. You step back onto the ball of one foot, rock backward while slightly lifting the front foot off the floor, and then shift the weight forward again onto the front foot. This step is performed in one count: "And ball, 1 change."

Three-step turn—This full turn is completed in three traveling steps. A turn to the right is executed by stepping on the right foot, then the left foot, and then the right foot again while making one complete revolution and traveling to the right. A turn to the left reverses the pattern.

Pirouette—This turn is executed on the supporting leg with the foot in relevé. The working leg is usually in a coupé or a retiré position and can be either turned out or in parallel. The turn can be performed either toward the supporting leg (inside, or en dedans) or away from the supporting leg (outside, or en dehors).

Chaînés—This chain of consecutive, traveling turns can be performed in demi-plié, on flat feet, or in a relevé position; parallel or turned out; and to the right or left. The feet step continuously one after the other. With each step, the body makes a half turn.

SAFETY TIP

Dancers "spot," or stare at something, while turning so that they can travel on a straight path and keep from growing dizzy. Some theatres even have a spotting light on the wall behind the audience for dancers to use.

Soutenu turn—This turn is used to change the position of the feet and travels very little. It can be performed in either direction and on relevé, flat feet, or in demi-plié. The working foot crosses in front of the supporting leg. As you do a complete turn in the direction of the supporting leg, the feet change position and the supporting leg ends up in front. This turn can also be done with the working leg crossing in back and the turn going toward the working leg. The step across is performed in one count, and the turn follows on the next count.

Sauté—A sauté is simply a jump. It can be performed on two feet or one. If a sauté is performed on one foot, it is a hop. When you do a sauté on one foot, the other leg can be in any position. A sauté can be performed turned out or in a parallel position.

Leap—In a basic leap, you jump off one leg while extending the other leg out in front of you. The leg you jumped off then extends out behind you, and you land on your front leg with the foot in demi-plié. A leap can be done by brushing the front leg or kicking it out in front of you.

Ballet Steps

Ballet began during the Italian Renaissance of the 15th century and eventually evolved into the classical dance form that we now know as ballet. Although dancers performed on their toes early in musical theatre dance history during the vaudeville era, classical ballet did not begin to appear in musicals until the 1930s when George Balanchine was hired to create the dances for *Ziegfeld's Follies* and *On Your Toes*.

Every step that is executed in ballet begins from one of the five turned-out positions. All the movements are performed with the legs outwardly rotated, and the vocabulary is all in the French language. Many of the standard steps are considered ballet steps when they are done in a turned-out position. Pas de bourrées, pirouettes, chassés, chaînés, soutenus, sautés, and leaps fall under the category of ballet when done turned out, and some of the steps may incorporate relevé. The following list describes some other basic ballet steps that will be helpful to you.

Ballet walks—These walks are performed in a turned-out position. You must fully extend the front leg before you step onto it. As you transfer the weight onto the front leg, the toes touch the floor first and you roll through the ball of your foot. Your heel is the last part of the foot to touch the floor. The back leg is in plié, and as you transfer the weight onto the front foot, the back leg pushes off the floor to propel you forward.

Bourrée—A series of quick, even steps done on demi-pointe or full pointe that gives the illusion of gliding across the stage. A bourrée can be done in any direction.

Tombé—The literal translation is "to fall." A tombé is a way to transfer your weight from one foot to the other. The leg that the weight is transferred to demi-pliés as it touches the floor. It often precedes a pas de bourrée.

Balancé—This step is a rocking step done in 3/4 time. You step either forward or to the side on the right foot. The left foot crosses behind it in a coupé position. You step on the left foot in demi-pointe as the right foot lifts slightly off the floor and then transfer the weight back onto the right foot again. It is then normally executed to the left starting with the left foot.

Waltz—Similar to the balancé, this step is also performed in 3/4 time. It is a traveling step that begins by stepping on the right foot as the left leg brushes or extends forward. You then take two steps forward on demi-pointe, first left and then right. The step is then typically repeated starting with the left foot.

Pique turn—In this turn you step onto demi-pointe on a straight leg and draw the other leg into a coupé or retiré position while turning. It can be executed in either a parallel or a turned-out position. If it is done in a turned-out position, the coupé or retiré is placed behind the supporting leg.

Jeté—The literal translation is "thrown." A jeté is any leap that transfers weight from one leg to the other.

Pas de chat—The literal translation is "cat step." This jump can be executed from either first or fifth position and is a traveling step. If you are traveling to the right, the right leg bends as you lift the foot to a retiré (back) position. As this foot begins to return to the floor, the left leg bends and you lift the left foot to a retiré (front) position before landing in the original position. When traveling to the left, the jump begins with the left foot.

Arabesque sauté—A hop on the supporting leg while the working leg is held in the arabesque position.

Jazz Steps

Jazz is a dance genre that was originally a combination of African dance and American social dance of the early 20th century. Exaggerated hip movements and foot stomping combined with country jig and clog dances to create jazz. Jazz also borrows from the genres of ballet, folk dance, modern dance, and tap dance. The body alignment and placement used in jazz comes from ballet, the upper torso isolations come from East Indian dance, its use of space comes from modern, and its rhythmic movements come from tap. Sometimes the term *show dance* is used interchangeably with the term *jazz dance*.

Although a turned-out position may occasionally be used, jazz technique is usually performed with the legs in parallel positions. A large portion of jazz choreography is composed of the turns and leaps mentioned earlier in this chapter. These turns and jumps are common to other dance forms as well, but when done as components of jazz, they are varied and embellished.

Turns—Although three-step turns, pirouettes, chaînés, and soutenu turns can be done with the arms held in traditional, classical positions and the torso and head held upright, the genre of jazz adds some variations to these positions. **Jazz hands** are often used; the palms of the hands face the audience, and the fingers are splayed open. At other times, the arms may be held in new, creative positions or may even change positions during a turn. Although in ballet most turns are executed in relevé, jazz choreography may require you to do turns in plié or move between demi-pliés and relevés during the same turn. Additionally, you may do turns with the torso in a **tilt**, a **contraction**, or in a **flat-back** position, and with a roll of the head. In contraction, the torso contracts inward so that the abdomen is hollowed out and the spine forms a C shape. The pelvis is pulled forward, but the shoulders remain over the hips. In a flat-back position, you bend forward from the hips at a 90-degree angle and hold the back straight and parallel to the floor. You should focus down and keep your neck in line with the rest of the spine. In a tilt, the back bends laterally to create an off-balance, asymmetrical position. It is often performed with one leg extended in second position.

Leaps—Traditional leaps are also embellished in jazz. Either one or both legs may be bent during a leap. Leaps may be done sideways in second position, or a jazz dancer may even perform a **scissor leap** in which the legs switch position in the air. A leap with the front leg bent so that its toes touch the extended back leg is called a **stag leap**, and a leap with one or both legs bent is called an **attitude leap**.

In addition to turns and leaps, other positions and movements specific to jazz are often included in musical theatre choreography.

Isolations—A main characteristic of jazz dance is that it uses body isolations. You will need to learn how to keep most of the body still while isolating certain parts. In jazz, dancers often move just the head, the shoulders, the ribs, or the hips.

Split—In a split one leg extends in front of the body while the other extends behind the body. A split can be a seated position on the floor or a position aimed for in a jump or leap.

Jazz split—In a jazz split one leg extends in front of the body while the other leg bends at the knee as the dancer slides to the floor.

> ### DID YOU KNOW?
>
> Bob Fosse (1927–1987) was a musical theatre dance choreographer known for creating dances characterized by many isolations. Some of his dances even required isolating the movements of the eyes or eyebrows.

Lunge—A lunge position is frequently used in jazz choreography. In a lunge the weight is shifted onto one leg that is in demi-plié and the other leg is held straight. Lunges can be performed to the front, the side, or the back.

Fan kick—In this kick the working leg crosses in front of the body and moves in an arc up to create a half circle before coming down on the opposite side.

Jazz walks—These walks are similar to ballet walks in that the toe touches the floor first with each step. The dancer then rolls through the foot, and the heel touches the floor last. Jazz walks are done in demi-plié with long strides. Arms are usually used in opposition so that when you are stepping forward with the right foot, the left arm is extended to the front and the right arm is extended to the back.

Jazz runs—Jazz runs are jazz walks that are done quicker and cover more distance with each step. You should appear to be gliding across the floor.

Jazz square—In the jazz square step, your feet trace the shape of a square on the floor. To do a jazz square to the right, the left foot crosses in front, the right foot then steps back about 12 inches (30 cm) behind the left foot, the left foot steps 12 inches to the left of the right foot, and the right foot steps 12 inches in front of the left foot to complete the pattern. This step can be reversed by starting on the right foot.

Pivot turn—A pivot turn is used to change the facing of your body. It can be executed as a quarter turn or a half turn. The working leg steps forward, and the supporting leg remains in place as the pivot point. The feet remain in this position as you turn your body by rotating on the balls of your feet.

Hitch kick—A hitch kick begins in a lunge position. The back leg brushes forward, and as you jump into the air, the second leg brushes forward while the first leg is coming down for you to land on in a demi-plié. During this jump, the legs pass each other in a scissor-like manner. A hitch kick may also be performed with the first leg coming to a bent position and the second leg brushing straight or to the back, with both legs brushing backward instead of forward.

Tuck jump—For a tuck jump, you step out on one foot while the other foot bends up under the body. To complete the jump, you then bend the other foot up under the body so that both legs are in a tucked position at the same time. Both feet land at the same time in demi-plié. This jump is done in a parallel position.

Social Dance Positions and Steps

This genre of dance has its roots in early courtship dances. Social dances are partner dances; they reflect our need to be socially connected to others. Ballroom dance is one form of social dance, as are contemporary partner dances like the tango and the Lindy. When used in choreography, the steps will be true to form, but social dances may be altered some because they are used in a performance setting and need to keep the audience involved.

Basic Partner Positions

Six basic partner positions are used in social dances. These **basic dance positions** determine how you relate to your partner during the dance. The man stands on the left side, and the woman is always on the right side in all these positions.

Shine position—In this position, the partners face each other without touching (figure 5.26).

Two-hands joined position—Partners stand facing each other. Both the man and the woman hold their elbows by their sides with their forearms extended (figure 5.27). They can both have their palms facing down, and the man can place his thumb in the woman's palm and wrap his fingers around the top of her hands, or the man can have his palms facing up and place his thumb on top of the woman's fingers and his fingers in her palm.

One-hand joined position—This position is the same as the two-hands joined position except that each partner uses only one hand (figure 5.28).

Figure 5.26   Shine position.

Figure 5.27   Two-hands joined position.

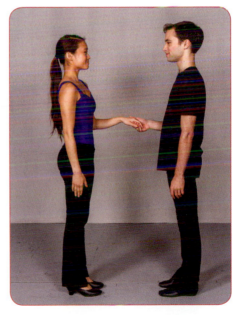

Figure 5.28   One-hand joined position.

Closed position—The partners face each other in this position. The man's left hand holds the woman's right hand. Palms are touching, and fingers and thumbs are loosely clasped around each other's hands. The man's right hand rests on the woman's back, cradling her left shoulder blade. The woman's left arm rests on top of the man's right arm, and her left hand rests gently on his right shoulder (figure 5.29).

Semiopen position—In this position, the partners stand beside each other with their bodies turned at a 45-degree angle to each other. The man places his right hand below the woman's left shoulder blade with his elbow slightly bent. The woman's left arm rests gently on the man's right arm, and her left hand is in front of his right shoulder. Both partners extend their outside arms and hold hands (figure 5.30).

Figure 5.29 Closed position.

Inside-hands joined position—The partners stand side by side. The man extends his right arm and offers his right hand to his partner, and the woman places her left palm in the man's right hand. Both place their outside hands on their hips (figure 5.31).

Figure 5.30 Semiopen position.

Figure 5.31 Inside-hands joined position.

Basic Steps

In social dance, basic movements are connected in recurring patterns to create the dances. Because social dances are partner dances, someone always leads the movement, typically the male, and someone follows, typically the female. The lead usually begins the steps on the left foot, and the person who is following uses the right foot to begin the patterns. Here are some of the common steps you will need to know.

Step hop—For a step hop you step from one foot onto the other, shifting your weight, and then hop on that foot.

Triple step—In this step you take three steps in two counts. You step on the right foot, then step on the ball of the left foot, and conclude with another step on the right foot. This step is counted "1 and 2." A series of triple steps are often done together and in various directions.

Rock step—In this step you transfer weight from one foot to the other with a rocking motion. You step backward on one foot with a full transfer of weight and complete it by stepping forward on the other foot while again transferring your weight. The rock step can also be done by rocking and stepping forward with the first foot and then stepping back onto the second foot. Each step receives a full count.

Box step—This six-count step makes a box, or square, pattern on the floor. The lead starts with the left foot stepping forward. A step to the side with the right foot follows, and then the left foot steps in to meet the right foot. The right foot then steps back, the left foot steps side, and the right foot steps in to meet the left. The person following begins with the right foot stepping backward and reverses the pattern.

Folk Dance Steps

Folk dance is a genre of dance that follows traditional or cultural norms. These celebratory or ceremonial dances are passed down through generations in different countries. Much like social dance, when they are performed under the genre of musical theatre dance, they may be altered slightly to be more interesting for the audience to watch. The following are some basic folk dance steps that will be useful to you.

Step—In this movement the weight is transferred from one foot to the other.

Stamp—A downward movement of the foot that does not transfer weight but makes a sound.

Heel and toe—The heel of one foot touches the floor, and the toe of the same foot then touches the floor.

Do si do—This movement begins with two dancers facing each other. They pass by each other by passing right shoulder to right shoulder, pass each other back to back, and then return to their original positions by passing left shoulder to left shoulder. During a do si do, the dancers stay facing the same direction the entire time.

Polka—This three-step movement begins with a hop. Beginning with the weight on the right foot, you hop on the right foot and then step left, right, left. You then reverse the step, hopping on the left foot and stepping right, left, right. It can travel in any direction. It is counted "and 1, 2, 3 and 1, 2, 3."

Schottische—This step moves sideways and is similar to the polka step, but the hop is at the end of the movement. Step the right foot out, step together with the left foot, step out with the right foot, and hop on the right foot. The step is then reversed, starting and ending on the left foot. It is counted "1, 2, 3 and 1, 2, 3 and."

Waltz step—This step is done in 3/4 time and is the same as the box step used in social dance.

PARTNERING AND LIFTING

No matter what form or style of dance a show might require, you will at times find yourself dancing with a partner and being expected either to lift the other dancer or to be lifted. Trust and communication are essential elements when dancing with another person.

Establishing a Relationship

When working with a partner, you need to build a relationship in which you trust each other completely. If partners do not trust each other, each will be constantly battling the other to remain in control, and the dancing will be tense and difficult for both dancers. Dancers who learn to trust each other feed off each other's energy, are able to work together creatively, and dance together smoothly and fluidly.

Partners also need to communicate with each other constantly. Establishing and keeping eye contact with your partner will allow you to coordinate the timing of dance steps and lifts. Letting your partner know whether a particular step or lift feels right or not is important in ensuring that the dance looks good and can be done safely.

Lifting Techniques and Safety Considerations

Lifts are exciting for an audience to watch and fun for dancers to perform. Besides developing a relationship with your partner and establishing trust, you need to remember some other things to keep you safe when you are lifting or being lifted.

If you are lifting another dancer, you must use your legs and arms to do the lifting and engage your abdominal muscles so that you will not strain or injure your back. Using a demi-plié before doing each lift will allow you to use the strength in the large muscles of your legs to complete the exercise. You also need to be sure that your partner is close to you. When your partner is too far from you, you have no control of the lift. Hand position is important when lifting a partner. For lifts in which you are standing behind your partner, your hands will be around your partner's waist right under the ribcage. Your fingers will be around the front of the torso, and your thumbs will be supporting your partner's back. If the two dancers are facing each other, the dancer doing the lifting will have his fingers on his partner's back.

If you are being lifted, remember that you need to help your partner. Dancers are not simply lifted. Some type of jump usually precedes a lift to provide the momentum that your partner needs to lift you. You also want to be sure to engage actively and use all your muscles as you are being lifted. Your partner helps and supports you but does not carry all your weight or determine where your body is in space.

The following are some basic lifts used in musical theatre dance:

Sauté lift—In this lift the person being lifted can be in a variety of positions. The feet can be in any dance position, and the lift can be performed with one leg in coupé, retiré, arabesque, or extended to the front or the back. The dancer being lifted begins with a demi-plié and jumps straight up, holding the position. She demi-pliés as she is lowered to the ground. The dancer who is doing the lifting places his hands on his partner's waist and demi-pliés with his partner. As she jumps, he extends his legs and lifts her into the air with his arms, supporting her and increasing the height of her jump. As he lowers her to the ground, he also demi-pliés to avoid straining his back.

Grand jeté lift—The dancer being lifted begins with one leg in demi-plié, executes a leap forward, and lands on the other leg in a demi-plié. The dancer who is doing the lifting places his hands on the waist of his partner, demi-pliés, and lifts her as she leaps, supporting her and increasing the height of her jump. As he lowers her to the ground, he also demi-pliés to avoid straining his back. A variety of steps might precede this type of lift, such as a dance run, a glissade, a chassé, or a pas de bourrée. The dancers must work together to coordinate the timing of this lift using the preceding step.

Seated shoulder lift—In a shoulder lift the lifter places his hands on his partner's waist. Both dancers demi-plié. The dancer being lifted jumps as her partner straightens his legs and lifts her to sit on his shoulder. The dancer being lifted must keep her back straight and engage her core muscles to keep herself straight and balanced while sitting on her partner's shoulder.

Dancers practicing a shoulder lift.

COMBINATIONS

The second half of each class will likely be spent learning how to apply what you have learned during the warm-up and center work. You will spend time learning to adapt dance steps to the musical theatre stage and learning dance combinations from a variety of shows.

After being introduced to new steps and movement in the first half of the class, you will learn to focus on executing the movement in the second half of class. Dance can play many roles in a musical. It can be used to express or change a mood or emotion, to generate energy, to add humor, to entertain, to develop a character, to help tell the story, to create a fantasy or dream sequence, or to serve as a celebration. Additionally, dance can complement the music.

Your teacher may select a few basic steps and challenge you to perform those steps in different ways, changing your purpose every time. For example, a jazz square can be done as a clown might do it to add humor to a production, in a militaristic fashion to create a tense mood, or in a quick, skipping manner to act as a celebratory movement.

You will probably spend several classes learning, rehearsing, and performing a specific combination. Your teacher will select a show that uses the form or forms of dance you have been studying in class and teach you a dance sequence from the show.

Besides learning and remembering the choreography, you will be asked to think about why that dance is part of the show. How and why does your character in the musical perform this dance? Depending on your response, you will be asked to perform the choreography in a manner that keeps that focus in mind. Eventually, you will be asked to sing at the same time if the scene requires it.

After learning the combination and perfecting it, the class will be divided up into groups, and you will have the opportunity to perform for your classmates. You can learn a lot by watching others, and you will often have the chance to offer constructive suggestions to each other to improve your performances. When you are the observer, you need to be attentive and polite, applaud your classmates' efforts, and offer feedback in a positive manner. Performing in front of others is challenging for everyone. Your class should be an environment in which everyone feels safe and can trust each other. This type of environment encourages you and your classmates to experiment while performing and to grow through your study of musical theatre dance.

SUMMARY

The musical theatre dance class is divided into sections that work together to help you learn as much about dance as you possibly can. Besides preparing you both mentally and physically for the class, the warm-up begins to make you feel comfortable with your body. The center work teaches you steps that you will likely use in the dance combination you will be learning that day. Learning and performing that combination for your peers will help you understand how to use the knowledge from class and translate it onto the musical theatre stage.

To find supplementary materials for this chapter, such as learning activities, e-journal assignments, and web links, visit the web resource at **www.HumanKinetics.com/BeginningMusicalTheatreDance.**

Chapter 6

From the Audition to the Stage

You have spent your time in the studio learning new vocabulary, learning about the ways your body can move, practicing steps, and performing combinations over and over again. All your hard work and newly gained experience will be put to the test as you begin to audition for shows. Although you will probably be nervous, arriving prepared and knowing what to expect will make your audition experience easier. Even if you do not get a role, each audition can be exciting. You will meet new people, learn to appreciate the talents of others, and find ways to improve yourself as a musical theatre dancer.

AUDITION PROCESS

If you have never before attended an audition, the experience can be daunting. The audition is the musical theatre performer's interview for a job. You need to think about how you present yourself and what impression you will make on your potential future employers—the director, music director, and choreographer. Take the time to do your homework to prepare for the audition. You should do some research and know the show for which you are auditioning. Several online resources offer synopses of shows, and online videos can give you a sense of the style of singing and dancing that the show will require.

Types of Auditions

The various types of auditions each serve a particular purpose. Knowing the type of audition you are attending will help you know what to take with you and how you should prepare. You should remember that the audition starts the minute you enter the building and does not end until you exit the building. Although you may only be milling around and getting ready, the production staff may already be watching how you move and interact with others to determine whether you might be a good fit for the production.

Cattle Call

The **cattle call** is an audition that is open to everyone. Depending on the type of production and theatre group for which you are auditioning, quite a few people could be auditioning. Although the audition may have specific requirements listed on the audition notice, you should generally be prepared to sing and deliver a short monologue. The best approach is to choose two pieces of music. One song should be an emotional ballad, and the other should be an up-tempo piece that shows your sense of rhythm. The monologue you choose should showcase your acting abilities and strengths.

Callback

The **callback** is an audition that you are invited back to so that the production staff can look at you a second time and gain a better understanding of who you are and what your talents and abilities are. At the callback you may be asked to read additional monologues, do a **cold reading**, or **improvise**. For a cold reading, you are asked to read from a script without having previously seen the material. If a director asks you to improvise, you will be required to act out a scene or situation spontaneously.

> **TECHNIQUE TIP**
>
> You should wear the same outfit for the callback as you wore to the cattle call to help the production staff remember you.

Dance Audition

The dance audition is usually held separately. Depending on the show and the amount of dancing required, it can be held at the cattle call or at the callback. You will be asked to learn one or more dance combinations from either the choreographer or a dance assistant. The combination will be in the form and style of the dancing that the show requires. You will be taught the combination with others who are auditioning. While you are learning it, you will want to position yourself so that you have enough room to dance without encroaching on anyone's personal space and so that you can see the person teaching the phrase. You will then be asked to perform it in a smaller group or perhaps even by yourself. Although you may practice the phrase while others are performing it, you must stay out of the performance space while others are taking their turns. The choreographer will be looking to determine your understanding of the presented material and the level of your dance training, to see how quickly you can learn the phrase, and to see how well you can perform the phrase. Your goal for the audition is to show the production staff your talents and abilities, so you should never hide in the back.

Attending the Audition

Knowing the show and having a thorough understanding of the theatre group for which you are auditioning will help you determine what to wear to the audition and what you should bring with you.

Because the audition is your interview, your clothing should be formal enough to make a good impression but casual enough for you to be comfortable when moving in it. You will also want to have dance clothes and a variety of dance shoes in your bag for the dance portion of the audition. You can never be certain what type of dance you will be asked to do, so you need to pack all the types of dance shoes you have.

ACTIVITY

PERSONAL SPACE VERSUS GENERAL SPACE

General space is the area within a dance studio or performance space in which you are able to move around. Everyone in the class, audition, or rehearsal shares this space. Personal space, however, is different. You need to establish your own personal space and be respectful of the personal space of others. To determine your personal space, stand in a wide second position and without moving your feet, use your arms to reach out into the space around you—the space above your head, the space down by your feet, and the space on all sides of and behind your body. This bubble of space you have explored around you is your **kinesphere**. Rudolf Laban came up with this label as he studied and analyzed movement. This kinesphere is your personal space.

You should be dressed neatly, and your hair should be neat as well. You should be able to pull your hair back and off your face for the dance portion of the audition. You should remove jewelry as well. The audition space is similar to the studio space used for class. You should not carry any food or drink into the space, and you should avoid smoking, chewing gum, or using your cell phone during the audition.

Arrive early for the audition to allow ample time to get through the registration process, prepare mentally, and warm up physically for the audition.

> ### DID YOU KNOW?
>
> The theatre world is a small one, and the impression you make at an audition or in your first show could follow you around for a long time. Jazz choreographer Jack Cole (1911–1974) was quoted as saying, "If you have a bad reputation from previous shows—late for rehearsals, irritability, laziness—you may be sure your case history is on file."

If you are auditioning for a professional company, bring a headshot and a resume to the audition. Your resume should include your contact information, your height, your weight, and a list of your professional experience and training. You should list your musical theatre performing experience first, followed by any theatrical performing experience you might have. You will then want to list your training and any professional workshop experiences in voice, acting, and dance. Your workshop experiences might include master classes you have attended or daylong conferences that included classes or lectures in music, dance, or acting. The final thing on your resume should be any special skills you might have like additional languages you speak, instruments you can play, or special performance tricks you might do such as acrobatics, baton twirling, or ventriloquism. Your resume should be no longer than one page, and you should be completely honest. The theatre world is small, and directors and choreographers talk to each other all the time. Any lies or exaggerations on your resume can be easily discovered and could cost you a role and destroy your reputation in the theatre world.

When you introduce yourself at the audition, be sure to make eye contact with the members of the production staff who will likely be seated in the house if the auditions are held in an auditorium or behind a table if the auditions are held in a room. Speak your name loudly and clearly. You should be polite and display a positive attitude from the beginning of the audition process until the end, when you should be sure to thank the staff for their time.

After the Audition

After the audition, your job is to go home and wait. You may receive a callback or a role in the show, or you may not. You can never be certain about what a director may be looking for when casting a show. You may be one of the most talented people who auditioned, but if the director is looking for a blond and you have brown hair, you are unlikely to be chosen. Keep in mind that often many people audition for a small number of roles and that the musical theatre world is competitive.

You may have to audition many times before you receive even a callback, but you should use each audition as an opportunity to gain experience and learn more about the audition process and yourself. By being able to step back and critique your performance at each audition, you will be able to improve your next audition.

When you do get a role in a show, you will begin a completely new adventure, making all the hours spent studying, practicing, and working hard seem worthwhile.

> **DID YOU KNOW?**
>
> When auditions were held for the Broadway musical *Cats*, 1,500 people auditioned for 26 roles.

THEATRE PROTOCOLS, ETIQUETTE, AND SAFETY

In class you have spent time learning about musical theatre dance. You have practiced steps and danced combinations over and over again. You have conquered your nervous fears and auditioned countless times. You have finally been called back and been told you have a role. So now what? After doing all that training, you now need to know the rules of the theatre. You need to understand the expectations of the directors, theatre etiquette, the language of the theatre, and the theatrical hierarchy. The more familiar you are with all this, the more positive and successful the opportunity will be for you.

Your audition was clearly successful, and the directors have seen something they like in you. Attending your first rehearsal will be an exciting new adventure, but you will need to be prepared. Knowing what is expected of you and how you should behave will make this new experience a fulfilling one.

Choreography that places dancers in close proximity to each other requires meticulous rehearsal.

Theatre Protocols and Etiquette

Your first rehearsal will probably be a **read-through** during which everyone gathers and looks at the script for the first time. Each actor will read her or his part aloud to get a better understanding of the show. At this read-through you will receive a rehearsal schedule and be introduced to all the members of the production staff.

You will be expected to arrive early to this rehearsal and all subsequent rehearsals. Your **call time**, or the time when you are asked to be at rehearsal, is the time you need to be ready to go, not arriving. When you enter the rehearsal space, you will need to prepare yourself both mentally and physically just as you have before every dance class and audition. You will need time to warm up your body, focus on the material you will be covering, and review any material that has been covered during previous rehearsals. Because you need to do all this preparation to have a successful rehearsal, arriving when you are called will be seen as arriving late. The posted rehearsal time is the time the director expects to begin working, not the time he or she expects everyone to be arriving.

There will normally be a **call board**, which is a bulletin board on which you will find such things as contact information, rehearsal schedules, rehearsal time changes, and notes from the production staff. It may also have a sign-in sheet for each member of the cast. You need to be sure to sign in and check this board for information and announcements. If you do not check the board and miss a rehearsal or arrive at the wrong time, it will be your fault and you could be in danger of losing your role.

As rehearsals begin, you must be fully present 100 percent of the time. The theatre has no room for individual egos or extraneous drama. You must leave at the stage door any emotional difficulties you may be encountering in your life, as well as any negative attitudes. Turn off your cell phone. You need to be able to give the production staff your complete attention. Remember that you are working for them, so you need to be open to any ideas they have and be willing to do whatever they ask of you whether you agree with it or not. In theatre, there should be implicit respect for those in positions of authority.

The production staff may rehearse things endlessly or may want to experiment with various ideas and change things frequently. The job of the directorial staff is to create the best production possible. Your job is to be a team player, comply with their requests, trust their knowledge and experience, and make the staff's vision come to life.

Throughout the rehearsal process, **notes** will be given. Sometimes they will be delivered orally, and at other times they may be posted on the call board. Notes are constructive criticisms given to improve scenes and dances. You should use them to better your performance; never take them

> ### TECHNIQUE TIP
> Be considerate of others at all times. Do your homework and come prepared for every rehearsal. Use your manners, be appreciative of others, and offer help and encouragement to your peers.

personally. By listening closely to the notes as they are given and implementing any changes requested, you will be making everyone's job easier and contributing to the progress and improvement of the production. If notes are given orally, you should nod and acknowledge the staff member giving the notes by saying, "OK," or "Thank you."

Theatre Safety

The theatre environment is much like that of the dance studio. Rules are in place to ensure safety and to make the experience positive for everyone.

You should come to rehearsals dressed appropriately and with the required dance shoes. Be sure that your hair is pulled back and away from your face and that you are not wearing any dangling jewelry that could pose a safety hazard to yourself or others.

Be aware of personal hygiene at all times. You will be spending many hours in small rehearsal spaces with fellow cast members. Bathing regularly, using deodorant, and washing your rehearsal clothes regularly are an important part of keeping the rehearsal environment pleasant for everyone.

No food or drink, other than water, should be in the rehearsal space. Dropped food or spilled drinks pose a safety hazard, so food and drink should be stored elsewhere during the rehearsal. Additionally, you should never chew gum during a rehearsal because it poses a choking hazard, could fall on the floor and cause an injury or a mess, and is not conducive to singing or delivering lines.

Most important, you should never use drugs or alcohol before or during any rehearsals or performances. These substances interfere with your ability to function optimally and could be dangerous to yourself or others should you not be able to rehearse and perform appropriately.

THEATRE STAFF AND HIERARCHY

You may now have a good idea about what your job is during rehearsals and performances. Now you need to understand how the entire staff works together to create a performance. Understanding the various jobs within a production and the hierarchy will be important so that you are aware of who is in charge of the elements that come together to create a cohesive and successful production.

The main production staff is made up of a producer, a director, a music director, a choreographer, a technical director, and a wardrobe and makeup director.

Producer

The **producer** oversees all parts of the production and ensures that everything runs smoothly. The producer acts as the business manager of the production and is therefore in charge of creating and following the budget; fund-raising; setting performance dates, times, and ticket prices; marketing and publicizing the show; creating a timeline for the rehearsal and production period in collaboration with the director; securing rehearsal and performance spaces; and hiring and overseeing the stage manager and house manager.

Stage Manager

The **stage manager** is in charge of scheduling, giving cues, taking notes, and communicating with the cast and designers during the rehearsal period. During the show, the stage manager is responsible for overseeing each performance. She or he is in charge of every scene change and is expected to be sure that all actors are where they need to be at all times. The stage manager is always listened to and respected because she or he is in charge after performances begin.

House Manager

Although the stage manager is in charge of everything that happens backstage, the **house manager** oversees everything that happens on the other side of the curtain. The house manager is responsible for the box office, everything that happens in the lobby, everything that happens in the audience, and the custodians. He or she must hire and oversee the people who run the box office, act as ushers, and sell souvenirs or serve refreshments in the lobby. Any time a problem arises in the audience such as a dispute over a seat or a loud, disruptive audience member, the house manager is called on to resolve the issue.

Director

The director controls all the artistic elements of the show. She or he is responsible for running the audition; casting the show; **blocking**, or staging, all the scenes; coaching the actors on line delivery; and helping with character development. The director is responsible for developing the concept behind the play and being able to explain it to the other members of the artistic staff and the cast. She or he must collaborate with the staff and be able to integrate all the acting, singing, and dancing in a seamless manner.

Music Director

The music director is responsible for working with both the cast and the musicians who will be playing in the orchestra for the show. He or she interprets the music and helps guide the director and choreographer by suggesting changes in the music or places where the music should be lengthened or cut shorter. The music director's jobs include securing rehearsal accompanists; hiring the **pit orchestra**, the group of musicians who will play the music during the actual performance; and rehearsing the music with the cast and the orchestra.

Choreographer

The choreographer is the movement expert. She or he is responsible for reading through the script, listening to the show's music, and developing movements and gestures that combine to create the show's dances. The choreographer is generally responsible for creating dance sequences, teaching them to the cast, and rehearsing them. She or he is also often responsible for adding gestural movement to other scenes and helping to block crowd scenes. The choreographer must make sure that acting can be conveyed through the selected movements and that the cast members are able to sing while dancing. Therefore, she or he must work closely with both the director and the music director.

Besides reading through the script and listening to the music, the choreographer must research the historical era of the show to be sure that the dances are appropriate for the setting of the musical. Many shows are set in a specific period, and the choreographer's movements should reflect the setting. For example, *The Boyfriend* is set in the 1920s when the Charleston was a popular dance. Using a dance from another era would not make sense or seem authentic.

A cast member is usually assigned the title of **dance captain**. The dance captain works under the choreographer and acts as her or his assistant. The dance captain is responsible for learning all of the choreography and helping other cast members learn it. He or she is required to teach choreography to replacement cast members and may be required to call and run additional rehearsals to practice choreography and give notes to cast members.

Technical Director

The **technical director** oversees all the technical aspects of the production. She or he works closely with the director to help create the mood of the production and be sure that the actors will be safe, seen, and heard. She or he is responsible for hiring a **scenic designer**, a **lighting designer**, and a **sound designer**. The scenic

Lighting effects can help direct the audience's attention and create a mood for the dance.

designer is responsible for creating a set that will work well in the performance space and help create the director's vision. He or she must work closely with the lighting designer, whose job it is to use lighting to ensure that all areas of the stage and the performers are visible at the right times, to set the mood, to direct the audience's attention, and to indicate the time of day during scenes. The sound designer is responsible for being certain that performers and musicians can be heard, that the sound is balanced in the theatre, and that all necessary sound effects are in place.

Although the director, music director, and choreographer all begin their work at the beginning of the production, most of the technical staff do not begin their work in the theatre until a few weeks before opening night. The people creating the set begin designing and building it early in the rehearsal process, but the lighting and sound crews will first enter the theatre during **load-in**, when lights are hung and wires for lighting and sound are run throughout the theatre.

Wardrobe and Makeup Supervisor

The **wardrobe and makeup supervisor** oversees the areas of both costume and makeup design. Responsibilities include researching the musical, meeting with the director and choreographer and working with the costume designer to ensure that the costumes will work well in all the scenes and still match the vision, determining what type of makeup will be used, measuring the actors and being certain that costumes fit well, and being certain that the costumes are laundered, ironed, and ready for each dress rehearsal and performance. Additionally, she or he is responsible for the storage of costumes and the physical transportation of them to and from the theatre.

> ### DID YOU KNOW?
>
> A **swing** is a member of the cast who is required to understudy many roles in the production so that he or she may immediately assume responsibility for a role should a fellow actor be unable to perform.

PREPARING TO TAKE THE STAGE

As opening night grows closer, rehearsals intensify, and the choreographer and director will become more demanding. This time, however, is exciting because everyone's hard work comes together to create a collaborative piece of art.

The two weeks before a show opens are the busiest for everyone involved in the production. Everyone is preparing for what will need to be done on opening night, and you will be involved in musical rehearsals with the live musicians, technical rehearsals, and dress rehearsals.

Musical Rehearsals

The first rehearsal of the cast and musicians is a rehearsal unlike any other. For the first time, the actors will hear the full orchestration and the musicians will hear the vocals sung with their playing. Up until this point, the musical numbers will likely have been rehearsed with only a pianist or with a recording. The **sitz**

probe, translated from German as "seated rehearsal," is the name given to this first rehearsal at which the cast and musicians sing and play through the entire show without any of the blocking or staging.

After this "getting acquainted" rehearsal, the musicians and cast will continue to work together as the show is continually run from beginning to end so that everyone begins to understand and grow comfortable with cues and tempos.

Technical Rehearsal

During **technical rehearsals**, the lighting and sound design are put together with the acting, singing, and dancing. The two types of technical rehearsals are a dry tech rehearsal and a tech rehearsal.

During a **dry tech rehearsal**, the entire technical crew is present but the performers are not. The technical crew runs through the show and has the opportunity to use the equipment and become familiar with the sequence of the show. Sound effects can be tested, and sound levels can be set.

After the dry tech takes place, everyone will attend the **tech rehearsal**. During the tech rehearsal, the cast will run through the entire show from **cue to cue**. A **cue** is an indication that an entrance or exit will be made, a song will start, scenery will be changed, or a lighting change will occur. The cue could be an actor's line, a change in a song, or a particular movement. Because this rehearsal moves from one cue to the next, there will be a lot of starting and stopping for the cast members while lighting and sound cues are synchronized. This long and tiring rehearsal requires a lot of patience from everybody, but the tech rehearsal is necessary to ensure that every element of the show works in combination with the other elements.

Dress Rehearsal

After the technical rehearsals are over, you will have a **dress rehearsal**. During the dress rehearsal, all actors wear costumes and full makeup and make sure that their hair is the way it will be for the actual performances. This rehearsal allows the wardrobe and makeup supervisor to eliminate issues or difficulties with costumes and determine how and where quick costume changes will happen. At the same time, the cast can get used to performing in costume. Although the cast has probably been using rehearsal props, the real props that will be used during the performances are introduced during the dress rehearsals. Several dress rehearsals will probably be done to ensure that everyone is comfortable and that the collaboration that creates a musical theatre production is successful.

Opening Night

With the long hours of rehearsal and preparation behind you, you will find yourself face to face with opening night and all the nerves and jitters that accompany it. Just as you were expected to follow etiquette in musical theatre dance class and at rehearsals, you will be expected to follow performer etiquette during the run of the show.

There will normally be a full-cast preperformance warm-up that will involve a vocal warm-up as well as a physical warm-up. You should wear practice clothes for the warm-up. Some actors find it helpful to do their own personal warm-up exercises as well. A personal warm-up, however, should be in addition to the group warm-up and not serve as a substitution. You are part of a team when you are in a show and should act like a team player.

When the warm-up is completed, you should check that any props you may need are in place. You will then be asked to clear the stage so that the technical crews can prepare it for the beginning of the show. You should gather your things quickly and move out of the way of the tech crew as quickly as you can.

While in your dressing room, you should be respectful of your cast members and their belongings. Do not borrow anything without asking or assume that you can move someone else's things without asking. If you choose to listen to music while you are getting ready, be sure to use headphones so that you do not disturb anyone.

You need to stay hydrated and well nourished during a performance, but you should never eat when you are in costume, and the only acceptable drink when you are in costume is water. Eating or drinking after getting dressed carries too great a risk of food or drink being spilled on and staining or ruining a costume. You should try not to sit down after you are in costume because someone has probably spent hours steaming the costumes so that they do not appear wrinkled when you go out onto the stage.

As you get ready, the stage manager will let you know how much time you have before the show begins. She or he will tell you when the house is open, and call, "Half hour," "Fifteen minutes," "Ten minutes," "Five minutes," and "**Places**." The time that is called is the length of time you have before the show will begin. When "places" is called, you have to get where you need to be when the show begins. You

DID YOU KNOW?

It is considered bad luck to wish a theatrical performer good luck. Instead, the traditional remark is "Break a leg." Several explanations for the origin of this phrase have been offered. In early Greek theatre, audience members who enjoyed a performance would stomp their feet vigorously. The performers hoped that the audience members would stomp so enthusiastically that they would break their legs. In Elizabethan times, the audience would show their appreciation by banging their chairs on the floor. If the performance was a good one, the chair banging might result in a broken chair leg. Another possible explanation is that performers who received thunderous applause would have to return for many curtain calls. The curtains that flank the entrances on the sides of the stage are called legs. Every time performers would have to return to the stage for a curtain call, they would have to "break through" the leg.

should respond orally to the stage manager's call every time so that she or he knows you have heard the call. Your response should repeat what has been said and be followed with "Thank you." If the stage manager calls, "Five minutes, please," your response should be "Five minutes, thank you."

When you are called to places and are awaiting your turn to enter, you must never talk backstage or block the wings. You should recognize that the stage manager is in charge, and you must do anything she or he may ask.

Soon enough, you will hear the first notes of the orchestra, watch the curtain open, and have the opportunity to transport an audience to a magical place for a few short hours while doing something you love and being proud of all your hard work.

SUMMARY

The audition experience is an adventure unlike any other. You need to gather information about the show for which you are auditioning and showcase your talents at the audition. Presenting yourself professionally and knowing what you should expect and what is expected of you will help make the experience positive. Learning from each experience will make you a better performer and help you eventually move from the arduous audition process into the exciting rehearsal process.

Preparing for a show is exciting, but it takes hard work, talent, dedication, responsibility, and collaboration. Understanding how the process works and who is responsible for each piece will help you know what is expected of you. Taking time to learn about theatre etiquette, the theatrical hierarchy, and the work that happens behind the scenes as you move from the first rehearsal to opening night will add to your excitement and ensure a pleasant experience.

To find supplementary materials for this chapter, such as learning activities, e-journal assignments, and web links, visit the web resource at **www.HumanKinetics.com/BeginningMusicalTheatreDance.**

WEB RESOURCE

Chapter 7

History of Musical Theatre Dance

Musical theatre dance has a rich history. Because the genre of musical theatre dance serves as an umbrella for many other dance forms and styles, its historical background is eclectic as well.

Dance in theatrical productions began on Greek and Roman stages as early as 500 BCE and wound its way through history to evolve into the dance musicals we see on the stage and screen today. Although originally dance was used simply as an accompaniment to dramatic productions, to operas, and in morality plays, in the 19th century dance became its own entity in the spectacle and exhibitionist performances on minstrel and vaudeville stages. Soon, the men who created the dance portions of productions were given credit as dance directors and eventually earned the title of choreographers. These choreographers fought to integrate dance into the story line of musical plays and then became directors who secured the place of dance on the musical theatre stage through concept musicals and dance musicals. Table 7.1 presents a general timeline for the evolution of musical theatre dance.

Table 7.1 Significant Events in Musical Theatre Dance History

500 BCE–1000 CE	Greek and Roman dramas
1100–1500	Dance in morality plays
1600–1700	Dance in operas, English theatrical companies
1800s	Minstrels, burlesque, vaudeville
Early 1900s	Ragtime
1900–1920	*Ziegfeld Follies*, chorus girls, influence of black musical theatre
1920–1930s	Dance director era
1930s–1940s	Choreographer era
1940s–1950s	Integration musicals
1950s–1980s	Concept musicals
1990s–present	Dance musicals, revivals, return to vaudeville

ORIGINS OF MUSICAL THEATRE DANCE

The first dramas that included music and dance were presented by the Greeks in the 5th century BCE. Those dramas served as models for the Romans, who expanded the dance element. During the Middle Ages, groups of traveling actors used dance to tell stories, and during the 12th and 13th centuries, the Catholic Church staged dramas that included music and dance to reinforce morality lessons and bring Biblical stories to life. As the Middle Ages ended and the Renaissance began, Greek dramas were resurrected. Some of these dramas, like Monteverdi's *Orfeo* (1607), which was performed at the Gonzaga court, and Purcell's *Dido and Aeneas* (1689), which was performed in England, featured dance and movement sequences. Pantomime performances were also popular and included singing, acrobatics, clown acts, and dialogue as well as dance. The dancing included in these pantomimes was considered show dance and could be anything from classic hornpipe dances to tightrope dancing. Additionally, dance was used between acts of Shakespearian plays and was used to entertain audiences between the acts of John Gray's *The Beggar's Opera* in 1728. These dances usually featured an individual dancing alone or leading a group of dancers who performed some type of Scottish folk dance.

DID YOU KNOW?

The Romans created the first tap shoes by nailing bits of metal to the soles of their sandals so that the dance steps could be heard.

A recreation of a Greek games dance.

Musical Theatre Dance in Colonial America

Across the ocean in colonial America, theatre was kept alive by British acting troupes. *The Beggar's Opera*, which premiered in Europe in the 1720s, was New York's first documented musical performance in 1750. In 1767 the Theatre on John Street opened and became a main performance space in New York for the remainder of the 18th century. The comic opera *The Archers*, performed there in 1796, is considered the first American-born musical (Kenrick, 2011). During the Revolutionary period in America (1764–1789), some members of the Continental Congress voiced their opposition to theatres and play-going because those pastimes were considered scandalous and distasteful (Kenrick, 2011). This opposition led to several of the 13 colonies banning public performances, but try as people might, keeping others from dancing is difficult, and even legislation could not stop it. Between 1750 and 1843, white men in black face traveled around the country, performing songs and dances in circuses and as entertainment during play intermissions (Kenrick, 2011). These intermission performances eventually developed into full-length minstrel performances in the mid-1800s.

Minstrelsy and Vaudeville

Minstrel shows were black song and dance parodies born when traveling black-face performers named themselves the Virginia Minstrels and presented a full-length show in 1843. But those minstrel shows were not allowed on Broadway, which was considered New York's cultural center and was meant for the elite citizens who enjoyed operas and plays. The minstrel shows were performed at the Bowery, which was where the lower class gathered. During the minstrel era, which lasted into the early 1900s, dance steps were officially given names that were written down.

In 1866 a production called *The Black Crook* was scheduled to be performed in New York at Niblo's Garden. Meanwhile, a Parisian ballet company had been booked to perform at the Academy of Music. A fire at the Academy of Music led to a merger of the ballet performance with the production of *The Black Crook*. The result was a 5 1/2-hour play with added songs and dances. The songs and dances had no relationship to the plot, making the production a circus-like spectacle that showcased individual dancers wearing only tight-fitting bodices and tights. *The Black Crook* was the first production in the United States to run longer than a year, and it marked the birth of musical theatre in the United States.

The Black Crook paved the way for the burlesque and vaudeville shows of the late 1800s. The burlesque shows of this decade featured women who wore costumes that showed the shapes of their bodies. Their performances entertained the middle and lower classes and used music and dance to mock operas, plays, and

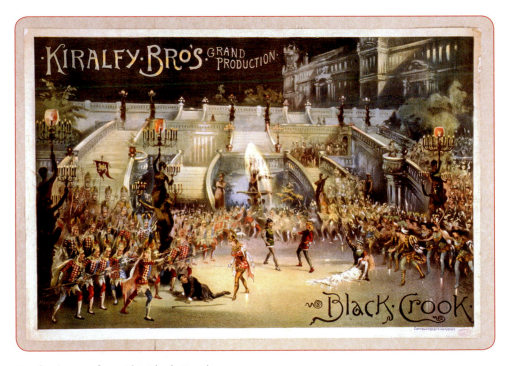

The final scene from *The Black Crook*.

the upper-class socialites. **Vaudeville** shows were a series of unrelated acts as part of an evening's entertainment that ignited interest in all kinds of dance, including Irish dance, clogging, tap, comic dancing, acrobatics, fancy dancing, skirt dancing, and toe dancing. Vaudeville was the training ground for people who would go on to perform in and create the Broadway musicals of the 20th century.

> ### DID YOU KNOW?
>
> The toe dancing done in vaudeville shows was very different from classical ballet dancing **en pointe**. It involved the dancers doing tricks, like jumping rope, while dancing on their toes. Some dancers even attached metal to the tips of their shoes to tap out rhythms while dancing.

Ballroom, Ragtime, and Chorus Girls

In the early 1900s, ragtime music, which combined European folk songs with West African drum rhythms, found its way onto the theatrical stage. The dance portions of performances began to expand. Dance directors gained recognition and focused on how the stage could be used and how the dances looked from an audience perspective. Additionally, dance instructors spent a lot of time training dancers to perform in specific ways. When **Vernon Castle** (1887–1918) and **Irene Castle** (1893–1969) refined and polished the dances that the black population had been doing to ragtime music, ballroom dancing was born. The Castles were responsible for making ballroom dance popular and altering those social dances to make them interesting for an audience to watch.

In the early 1900s, **John Tiller** (1854–1925) founded a school in London, England, that offered dance training to women, who became known as London's **Tiller Girls**. They were trained to perform in unison, to march in military formations with military precision. Tiller provided dancers for London's revues and musical comedies and brought girls to the United States to dance in vaudeville shows and musical plays like *The Man in the Moon* (1899) and *The Casino Girl* (1901). As time passed, he added can-can kicks and vaudeville-type steps to their training. Similar schools soon opened in the United States.

Ned Wayburn (1874–1942) founded the Studio of Stage Dancing in 1905 in Manhattan and created kick lines. Although he believed that all dancers needed to be trained, his first priority was appearance. Dancers were chosen for shows because of their beauty, and he was the first dance director to demand that all the dancers in his chorus line be the same height.

His dances contained intricate, fast steps, and he demanded musicality and smiles. Wayburn effectively used **tableaus**, or groups of posed, still dancers, to depict scenes on the stage. He was probably the most influential, successful, and best-known dance director of his time, acting as dance director for the *Ziegfeld Follies*, an annual show produced by **Florenz Ziegfeld** (1867–1932) from 1916 through 1919 and again from 1922 through 1923. He is credited with developing the Ziegfeld walk, which required the dancers to walk down stairs balancing enormous headpieces by simultaneously thrusting one hip forward and pushing the opposite shoulder forward.

A *Ziegfeld Follies* performer from 1925.

Also known for their work on the *Ziegfeld Follies* were dance directors **Julian Mitchell** (1854–1926) and **Albertina Rausch** (1891–1967). Mitchell expanded on Tiller's idea of the chorus girl and developed the concept of a grand production number. Mitchell was responsible for the dancing in both *The Wizard of Oz* in 1902 and *Babes in Toyland* in 1903.

Albertina Rausch was the third dance director of the *Ziegfeld Follies*. She brought elements of her classical ballet training to Broadway by combining ballet arm movements, or port de bras, similar to those used in classical ballet, with less stylized movements and by combining the eccentric vaudeville toe dancing with Tiller precision. She set this dancing to modern music and called it American ballet (Kislan, 1987).

Meanwhile, in Harlem, black musical theatre was also flourishing. Opening in 1911, *The Darktown Follies* was an all-black musical featuring a circle dance that involved everyone snaking around the stage with his or her hands on the hips of the next person in line. This circle dance was purchased by Florenz Ziegfeld to be used in his *Follies*. In 1923 the show *Runnin' Wild* reached back to the Ashanti dancers of Africa and featured one of their dances on stage, called the Charleston.

Lines between black and white musical theatre began to blur as the whites began to borrow more black dances and perform them on white stages.

During this period, dance went from being an accompaniment for stage plays to earning a featured place on the stage. Thanks to *The Black Crook* and notable dancers like the Castles, Ned Wayburn, Julian Mitchell, Albertina Rausch, John Tiller, and Florenz Ziegfeld, dance began to earn a more prominent place in performances.

DANCE DIRECTOR ERA

During the 1920s and 1930s, more dance directors contributed a combination of elements to choreography, which helped shape musical theatre dance. Many of these elements are still seen on stages today. **Bobby Connolly** (1897–1944) is credited with popularizing tap dance in chorus numbers and making tap the most popular stage and movie musical dance form from 1900 to 1930. In the 1920s, when the dance chorus and the singing chorus were completely separate from each other and dance was considered mainly a decorative part of musicals, a man named **Seymour Felix** (1892–1961) created dances that began to pantomime the plot and helped to tell a story. He used this technique in *Simple Simon* (1930). Felix was reported to be the highest paid dance director of his time.

As in the early 1900s, the gathering places for white people and black people remained segregated during this period. While the white men were gathering in bars called honky-tonks, African Americans were gathering in run-down shacks known as **juke joints**. Anyone looking inside a juke joint would see dancing that featured hip motions from the African Congo, upper torso pulsing that originated on the West African Coast, and footwork characteristic of the pygmy tribes of the African rainforests. All this authentic African dancing was combined with movements from European country jigs and clog dances to help shape American musical theatre dance.

The early 1900s focused on bringing dance to the forefront of performances, but the dance directors of this era began to experiment by adding and mixing dance forms and styles and straying from the conventional unison dancing that was characteristic of groups like the Tiller Girls and Albertina Rausch's dancers. This experimentation continued as dance directors became more important in productions, earning themselves the right to be given credit for their work and be called choreographers.

CHOREOGRAPHER ERA

The era of the choreographer began in the 1930s. Up until then, those who created the dances and worked with the dancing chorus were simply called dance directors, and before 1910, no one was even given credit in printed programs for creating and directing dances. This lack of acknowledgment changed in 1936 when **George Balanchine** (1904–1983) was hired to create the dances for *On Your Toes*. Balanchine trained at the Russian Imperial Ballet School and danced with Serge Diaghilev's Ballets Russes before coming to the United States. His main contribution to the musical theatre stage was the ballet "Slaughter on Tenth Avenue" from *On Your Toes* (1936) because it demonstrated how dance could be woven into the story line of a musical. This extended ballet helped advance the plot and develop the personality of a main character. Junior learns that he will be killed at the end of the dance unless he is able to continue dancing until help arrives. Although the

A scene from Balanchine's "Slaughter on Tenth Avenue."

dance begins with simple movements, the dancing grows frantic as it continues, showing the character's desperation. With the creation of "Slaughter on Tenth Avenue," Balanchine paved the road for the development of the integrated musical. Balanchine was also the first person to demand that he be billed as a choreographer. He went on to choreograph *Babes in Arms* (1937), which featured the Nicholas Brothers, African American tappers from the vaudeville circuit, *I Married An Angel* (1938), which included so much ballet that the lead was played by a professional ballerina, and *Boys From Syracuse* (1938). Although all these shows featured dance numbers, most were either dream ballet sequences or hoofing routines that, unlike "Slaughter," did not really help tell the story.

The 1930s also saw the inclusion of modern dance in some Broadway musicals. Charles Weidman used modern dance in the 1937 production of *I'd Rather Be Right*, a satirical play based on the life of Franklin Delano Roosevelt. Shortly thereafter, modern dancers Helen Tamiris and Hanya Holm left the modern dance world to become successful Broadway choreographers. Tamiris choreographed the revival of *Showboat* in 1946 and *Annie Get Your Gun* in 1954, and Holm was responsible for the dancing in *Kiss Me Kate* (1948) and *My Fair Lady* (1956).

Around the same time, **Jack Cole** (1911–1974), who had danced on Broadway in the 1930s, became the first Broadway choreographer to adapt ethnic dances for the musical theatre stage. His choreography was a mixture of ballet, modern dance, ethnic dance, and popular dance. He called his style urban dance, but others began calling it theatrical jazz dance because it was often set to jazz music. His strenuous and demanding dances were emotional showstoppers. Although he choreographed more than 20 shows on Broadway, none were considered hits. He became better known for his training of dancers like Gwen Verdon, who later became a Fosse dancer, and his work in movie musicals. He had a talent for making nondancers like Marilyn Monroe seem like amazing dancers on film thanks to his choreography and his knowledge of film editing. He is known for paving the way for jazz in theatre and film for future choreographers like Jerome Robbins, Bob Fosse, and Michael Bennett. Cole is known as the father of modern jazz dance (Levine, 2012).

Another dancer who combined different forms and styles of dance on stage and screen was ballet dancer **Robert Alton** (1902–1957). He used tap dance but added elements of ballet, ballroom, and ethnic dancing to keep the whole body moving. Alton worked to elevate the role that dance played in musicals, both on Broadway and in Hollywood. He had high standards, and his work in *Anything Goes* in 1934, in the original *Pal Joey* in 1940, and in its revival in 1952 related the dances to the song lyrics and encouraged audiences to pay attention to the dances.

INTEGRATION MUSICAL ERA

Before 1940 every actor in a musical was required to sing and dance. Thus far, the singing had not been demanding, and musical theatre choreography had consisted mostly of simple steps and kicks repeated in various patterns. The era of the integration musical changed that by making dance an essential part of the story line. Dances no longer served as breaks in the story solely to entertain the audience. Instead, the dances were used to continue the plot, and a new form of musical theatre was born.

The 1943 production of *Oklahoma!* was the first musical to use two separate groups of performers: 16 singers and 18 dancers were hired, thanks to a dancer and choreographer named **Agnes de Mille** (1905–1993). Acting as the show's choreographer, de Mille insisted on auditioning and hiring the dancers herself, and she used her dances to tell a story. *Oklahoma!* became the first musical to integrate the songs, the dances, and the story line. No breaks occurred in the dramatic action. The transitions between the dances and the story were seamless in all her Broadway work. The dances she created for *Brigadoon* (1947) blended so well that no definite times could be given for when dances began and ended.

De Mille considered her choreography to be playwriting, and she worked on creating imaginative movement that could help with character development. She found tap dance, ballroom, and acrobatic dancing to be limiting, so she began to create an interpretive dance style that was character driven. This style was a blend of ballet and interpretive modern dance. De Mille required dancers to act as well as move. Her use of diagonals created a strong sense of depth and perspective, and her dances were so strong that they could stand alone if the other elements of the musical were removed.

Agnes de Mille worked closely with music directors, rehearsal pianists, and music arrangers. In the past, dance music had simply been repeated snippets from the original score of a show. She demanded that music be composed as the dance took

Agnes de Mille as a cowgirl in her Western-based ballet *Rodeo.*

shape. Additionally, she required book writers and costume designers to adapt to her dance ideas. In *One Touch of Venus* (1943), she went as far as to demand that scenery be cleared from the stage to accommodate one of her dances.

Her choreography for *Carousel* in 1945 surpassed what had been seen on Broadway stages thus far. DeMille used a short 12 1/2 minutes to introduce a new character and deliver a synopsis of her life. One of the show's main characters, Billy Bigelow, had been killed before his daughter, Louise, was born. He is given the opportunity to look down from the gates of heaven at his adolescent daughter to determine how he might help her and gain entry into heaven through this good deed. The ballet is used to illustrate how Louise is bullied by her peers and unwittingly seduced by a member of a traveling circus. This dance sequence became a play within a play, without which the musical would make no sense. The musical also contained a 6-minute sailor's hornpipe. The research and work that de Mille did to create this dance made it look like a natural part of the sailors' everyday lives.

De Mille's strong personality and her demands on directors, theatrical staff, and dancers elevated the role of choreographer to a new level, and for a while she became the most powerful woman on Broadway and the single most important transitional figure in Broadway dance history. Thanks to her views and her willingness to fight for her work and her dancers, dance became an integral and respected part of the American Broadway musical.

CONCEPT MUSICALS
AND DIRECTOR–CHOREOGRAPHERS

Moving beyond song and dance musicals in which dance helped advance the plot and develop the characters, **Jerome Robbins** (1918–1998) introduced the **concept musical** in which everything unites to communicate a central theme or idea. Classically trained, Robbins was primarily a ballet choreographer. When his ballet *Fancy Free* was made into the musical *On the Town* in 1944, Robbins was called in to help save the subway scene because the staging was not working well. In this way, Robbins began his Broadway career. Because his training was mainly classical, Robbins spent many hours researching the historical background of musicals, studying the characters, and thinking about the motivation behind the dances.

He worked hard to make sure that the 16-minute Siamese dance in the 1951 production of *The King and I* that told the story *The Small House of Uncle Thomas* was authentic and ethnologically sound. The opening song "Tradition" from *Fiddler on the Roof* (1964) was choreographed to embody the entire Jewish culture. Robbins' work changed the face of Broadway.

Fiddler on the Roof revolved around Jewish traditions, and Robbins' 1957 production of *West Side Story* was based on the concept of street violence. The musical required strong dancers because movement was integral to the entire show.

Robbins was so involved in creating musicals that he eventually took on the task of directing as well, paving the way for others to do the same. He was a demanding director–choreographer who continued Agnes de Mille's mission and went even further. He continued the complete integration of singing, acting, and dancing through the 1954 production of *Peter Pan*, the 1959 production of *Gypsy*, and the 1962 production of *A Funny Thing Happened on the Way to the Forum* before leaving Broadway and returning to New York City Ballet at the age of 46.

Director–choreographer **Gower Champion** (1919–1980) also worked to integrate dance seamlessly into musicals. His goal was to blend everything together so that a show would flow smoothly and no dance steps would stand out. As a director–choreographer, he used ballroom dance and employed set pieces and props in dance numbers. He is responsible for the successful runs of *Bye, Bye, Birdie* in 1960, *Carnival* in 1961, and *Hello, Dolly* in 1964. *Bye, Bye, Birdie*'s choreography was the first to be preserved and recorded in Labanotation, a specialized, detailed form of dance notation that uses symbols on a vertical staff to indicate the body parts used, the timing of a movement, the level of a movement, and the direction in which

> ## DID YOU KNOW?
>
> Robbins needed a cast of skilled dancers for *West Side Story*, but because hiring both a group of singers and a group of dancers was too expensive, he had to hire skilled dancers who could act and sing adequately. Therefore, the music for *West Side Story* was written without voice parts, and everyone sang in unison.

Fosse demonstrating his iconic style.

the dancer is moving. At times, however, Champion's staging overshadowed the plot and made the musical numbers seem more important than the script.

Thanks to Agnes de Mille, Jerome Robbins, and Gower Champion, dance now occupied an important place in the musicals of this era. As the choreographers gained more control, they found it difficult and self-defeating to work with directors. The choreographers now also directed musicals, and Robbins helped usher in the era of director–choreographers. Director–choreographers used all types of dance on the stage, including tap, jazz, ballet, ballroom, and folk dance. This era developed a sense of unity in productions, elevated the role of dance in musicals, and provided more work for dancers.

During the 1950s a new director–choreographer named **Bob Fosse** (1927–1987) appeared on Broadway. Fosse performed in burlesque shows and nightclubs as a child, but his strong personality prevented him from being hired as a dancer on Broadway. He decided to become a choreographer, but his resistance to compromise led to his quickly becoming a director–choreographer. Fosse's choreography had a unique style. His dance numbers usually included dancers who wore white gloves and black costumes and used canes. When Fosse began losing his hair, he started wearing a hat all the time, so most of his dancers performed in black derby hats. Fosse was born pigeon-toed and had poor posture, which led to the development of his signature style. His dances feature bent knees, turned-in feet, limp wrists, and hunched shoulders, as well as small groups of dancers who moved across the stage together in a clump known as the Fosse amoeba.

The hip isolations, undulating shoulders, backward leans, and percussive movements of his dances in the 1955 production of *Damn Yankees* and "Steam Heat" from *Pajama Game* (1956) garnered public notice. Although he believed that all movements in a show should be similar, he also believed that dances should stand out. Many thought that after Agnes de Mille's and Jerome Robbins' efforts at creating integrative musicals, Fosse's razzle-dazzle style moved Broadway backward. His desire for his dances to be noticed led to disagreements with directors, who had different visions for how certain scenes should be staged.

Fosse was the choreographer of George Abbott's production of *New Girl in Town* (1957) until Abbott rejected some of Fosse's choreography. Fosse then vowed that he would both direct and choreograph all future shows on which he worked. He served as the director–choreographer for *Redhead* (1959), *Little Me* (1962), *Pippin* (1972), and *Chicago* (1975), and in 1966, he single handedly conceived, directed, and choreographed *Sweet Charity*.

Pippin was originally written as a cute, sentimental play within a play that portrayed the life of King Charlemagne's son, Pippin. Fosse, who had a reputation for producing dark theatre, cast himself as the devil, who led Pippin on a quest for personal fulfillment and changed the mood of the show. Fosse was also responsible for creating the first television commercial to promote a musical. His *Pippin* commercial showcased snippets of dance numbers and helped encourage the idea of dance as spectacle.

Chicago (1975) was based on a weak book without much of a plot, and it ended up being more like a vaudeville revue with spectacle-type numbers like "All That Jazz" and "Razzle Dazzle." Fosse's 1978 production of *Dancin'* was not based on a book at all; it was composed of newly choreographed dances to songs from the past.

The foremost director–choreographer of the 1970s concept musicals was **Michael Bennett** (1943–1987). His choreography shined in *Company* (1970) and *Follies* (1971), but his work in producing a show solely about dance and dancers, *A Chorus Line* (1975), was a celebration that ran on Broadway for 15 years. *A Chorus Line* was the first Broadway show to be cast and rehearsed *before* the book was written. The show was created in a series of workshops. It used the raw emotion expressed by Broadway dancers, who spoke about their lives in taped interviews. The choreography reflected the characters and their stories and created the basis for the book. Likewise, his 1981 production of *Dreamgirls* was developed through workshops. This show traced the history of black music from the 1960s to the 1980s. Bennett's dance-oriented shows used movement to convey universal themes to which audience members could easily relate.

The late 1960s and 1970s brought the productions of *Hair* (1968) and *Oh! Calcutta!* (1972) to the Broadway stage. Both shows contained nudity. During those years Times Square in New York City was becoming home to strip clubs, adult bookstores, drug dealers, and hookers. Broadway became a dangerous place to be, and many declared the Broadway musical dead.

TAP MUSICALS, REVIVALS, AND DANCE MUSICALS

Some saw the 1980s as a mediocre decade on Broadway, but the musical theatre stage saw a resurgence of tap dance in shows like Gower Champion's *42nd Street* (1980), *The Tap Dance Kid* (1983), and *Black and Blue* (1989). **Savion Glover** (1973–) worked hard to keep tap dance visible and continued to do so into the 1990s with *Bring in Da' Noise, Bring in Da' Funk* (1996). In that musical, Glover used tap and hip-hop to create a living history of African Americans, beginning with their voyages on slave ships and ending in 1995. His goal was to use tap to convey deep personal emotions and elevate its role from that of spectacle entertainment.

Graciela Daniele (1939–) also made sure that dance remained an important part of Broadway shows. Her training in ballet, modern, and jazz dance helped her create intricate dance numbers that used movement to tell stories that captivated the audience in *Pirates of Penzance* in 1981, *The Mystery of Edwin Drood* in 1985, and *Ragtime* in 1998.

The 1980s laid the groundwork for the continued use of dance in Broadway shows, and dance remained an important part of musicals during the 1990s era of the Broadway revival.

Revivals had always been part of Broadway's musical history. Popular shows were resurrected under new direction with new cast members and recreated to pay homage to the original productions while introducing younger audiences to the stories of the past. But during the 1990s, few original shows were being produced and Broadway seemed to be relying on revivals. Between 1995 and 1996, 55 percent of Broadway shows were revivals, as opposed to 33 percent between 1965 and 1966 (Long, 2001).

A new versatile, energetic, and ambitious director–choreographer named **Susan Stroman** (1954–) began to make a name for herself with her Tony Award–winning choreography in *Crazy for You* (1992) and in the revival of *Showboat* in 1994 and, as director–choreographer, for the 1999 revival of *Music Man*. Stroman was hired to choreograph a London revival of *Oklahoma!* in 1999, and some critics thought that her choreography surpassed that of Agnes de Mille.

Stroman served as a mentor for **Rob Marshall** (1960–) who choreographed during the 1990s and whose staging has been described as imaginative and new. He was the director–choreographer for the revivals of *A Funny Thing Happened on the Way to the Forum* (1996) and *Promises, Promises* (2010). He codirected the revival of *Cabaret* (1998), in which he turned the audience into the customers at the Kit Kat Club.

Similar to these revivals of the 1990s were the productions that showcased a collection of a choreographer's past work. Opening in 1989 was *Jerome Robbins' Broadway*, a show composed of recreations of Robbins' choreography from 1944 to 1964. Another example was *Fosse*, which opened in 1999. Produced by Anne Reinking and Gwen Verdon, *Fosse* paid tribute to the late director–choreographer.

Alongside these productions were dance-driven musicals that gained popularity near the turn of the century. Susan Stroman, who had made a name for herself working on revivals, directed and choreographed *Contact* in 2000. The show was composed of three danced miniplays set to prerecorded classical and popular music. The show had no orchestra, no singing, and no book, so people questioned whether it was truly a musical, yet it became the first dance show to win a Tony for Best Musical.

Modern dancer and dance company director **Twyla Tharp** (1941–) also helped usher in the era of the dance musical. In 2002 Tharp's dances, staged to popular music by Billy Joel, won the Tony Award for Best Choreography in the musical *Movin' Out*. Her 2006 dance musical *The Times They Are A-Changin'* combined singers and dancers onstage. In 2010 she wrote, choreographed, and directed *Come Fly Away*. This musical included dances she had choreographed in the 1980s to songs by Frank Sinatra.

MUSICAL THEATRE IN THE 21ST CENTURY

The 21st century ushered in a time when Broadway musicals were dance driven, but choreographers found contemporary ways to bring dance to the stage. Few original shows were produced, and musical theatre seemed to be feeding off other art forms. Shows like *Hairspray* (2002), *Never Gonna Dance* (2003), and *Spamalot* (2005) were recreations of movies. The stories were infused with song and dance numbers that seemed to materialize out of nowhere and bore little, if any, emotional connections to the story lines.

The arrival of the 21st century also brought spectacular technological advances to Hollywood movies that overshadowed the thrill of live performances, and high ticket prices on Broadway led to a decline in musical theatre audiences. Between 2002 and 2003, Broadway attendance decreased by half a million people. To help thwart this decline, musical theatre dance took a turn back toward the spectacle-type choreography of the vaudeville era. Many refer to this time as the Disneyfication of Broadway.

Corporate Musicals

When Disney began to produce shows, the **corporate musical** was born. Entertainment corporations built, produced, and managed the shows. *Beauty and the Beast* (1994), *The Lion King* (1997), *The Little Mermaid* (2008), *Newsies* (2012), and *Aladdin* (2014) were spectacles similar to those seen in Disney theme parks, complete with backflips, cartwheels, wheel-heeled shoes, and kick lines reminiscent of vaudeville acts.

Dance Musicals

The few completely new shows that came to Broadway contained show-stopping song and dance extravaganzas. Susan Stroman used props in innovative and creative ways in shows like *The Producers* (2001), which included a dance using walkers. Sergio Trujillo transformed the musical theatre stage to a modern-day *American Bandstand*. His recreations of the Mashed Potato, the Watusi, and the Twist, popular dances from the 1950s, brought *Jersey Boys* (2005) and *Memphis* (2009) to life.

In 2007 *In the Heights* choreographer **Andy Blankenbuehler** (1970–) merged street dance with athletic movements. Postmodern dance choreographer **Bill T. Jones** (1952–) brought Nigerian dance to the Broadway stage in *Fela!* in 2009. Ballroom dance was featured on the Broadway stage again in *Burn the Floor* (2009), and Steven Hoggett admirably integrated dance numbers set to music by the popular band Green Day into the show *American Idiot* (2010). In *Bring It On* (2012), Andy Blankenbuehler incorporated acrobatic and aerial stunts into cheerleading routines. In the 2013 production of *After Midnight*, Warren Carlyle, who had worked as Susan Stroman's assistant on *The Producers*, showcased dance that had dancers performing while cartwheeling and moving across the stage on their hands and backs. The more recent production of *Motown: The Musical* (2013) used dance to take the audience on a trip down memory lane through the 1960s and the 1970s. Although Susan

Stroman continued to feature dance in *Bullets Over Broadway* (2014), she too used a flashy gangster tap dance.

Choreographers like Bill T. Jones, Peter Darling, and Jerry Mitchell continued to integrate dance into story lines. For *Spring Awakening* (2006), Jones created dances described in a *New York Times* review as "neatly woven into the show's texture" (Isherwood, 2006). Darling's ballet choreography helped tell the story of *Billy Elliot* (2008). Dance critic Ben Brantley said that Jerry Mitchell, known for the earlier musicals *Hairspray* (2002), the 2004 revival of *La Cage Aux Folles, Legally Blonde* (2007), and *Catch Me if You Can* (2011), used movement to define the characters in *Kinky Boots*, a 2013 production about a struggling shoemaker and his drag queen business partner.

Although dance remained an important part of the Broadway musical during this period, it was brought to the stage through revivals, revues, and musicals that featured only dance. This change caused people to question the future of the Broadway musical. But spectacle-driven and corporate musicals appeared to reenergize Broadway audiences and carry the American Broadway musical into the new century.

SUMMARY

Musical theatre dance has a rich historical background. Its roots can be traced back to Greek and Roman dramas when dance was paired with music to tell a story. As time passed, dance became mainly a form of entertainment and served as spectacle. Eventually, thanks to many influential choreographers, dance competed for and earned a respected place within the Broadway musical. Integration musicals used dance together with music and acting to tell a story. In the 21st century, musical theatre dance seems to have reverted to vaudeville-type acts in which dance is an attraction to draw in the crowds. Special effects and 3-D movies have raised audience expectations, and a lot more is now needed to impress an audience. Only time will tell whether dance as spectacle in musical theatre productions will be what it takes to keep audience members coming to Broadway and keep musical theatre dance alive.

To find supplementary materials for this chapter, such as learning activities, e-journal assignments, and web links, visit the web resource at **www.HumanKinetics.com/BeginningMusicalTheatreDance.**

WEB RESOURCE

Glossary

Alton, Robert (1902–1957)—Ballet dancer who elevated the role of dance in musicals by relating the dances to the song lyrics.

arabesque—A balance in which one leg is extended to the back at 45 degrees or higher. Arm positions relate to the school or style of ballet.

arabesque sauté—A hop on the supporting leg while the working leg is held in the arabesque position.

arena stage—A performing space located in the middle of an auditorium and surrounded by bleacher-type seating.

artistry—Artistic skill or ability.

attitude leap—A leap in which one or both legs are bent.

balance—An aesthetic principle that focuses on making certain that all parts of the dance are proportional to each other. It provides a sense of equality.

balancé—A rocking step done in 3/4 time and used in ballet. The right foot steps either forward or to the side. The left foot crosses behind it in a coupé position. The left foot steps in demi-pointe as the right foot lifts slightly off the floor and the weight is transferred back onto the right foot again. It is performed in a waltz tempo and counted "1 and a."

Balanchine, George (1904–1983)—Cofounder of New York City Ballet who introduced classical ballet to the musical theatre stage. He was the first person listed as a choreographer in a playbill.

ball change—A rocking step that shifts weight using two steps in one count. A step on the ball of one foot on the "and" count is followed by a step on the other foot on the beat.

ballet walks—Walks performed in a turned-out position. You must fully extend the front leg before you step onto it. As you transfer the weight onto the front leg, the toes touch the floor first and you roll through the ball of your foot. Your heel is the last part of the foot to touch the floor. The back leg is in plié, and as you transfer the weight onto the front leg and foot, the back leg pushes off the floor to propel you forward.

basic dance position—A partner position used in social dance in which the partners face each other. The man is on the left, and the woman is on the right.

Bennett, Michael (1943–1987)—The foremost director–choreographer of the 1970s, he created concept musicals with universal themes to which the audience could easily relate. Best known for his work on *A Chorus Line* (1975) and *Dreamgirls* (1981).

Blankenbuehler, Andy (1970–)—Twenty-first century choreographer known for merging street dance with athletic movements on the musical theatre stage.

blocking—Staging a scene.

body circles—An exercise that warms up the upper body. Beginning with the body fully extended and the arms reaching straight overhead, you circle your torso to the right while reaching sideways, to the floor while reaching down and looking at your legs, to the left while reaching sideways, and back to your original position. The movement is then reversed, starting the circle to the left.

bone density—The amount of minerals in a given area of bone, which is an indicator of bone strength.

bourrée—A ballet step that is a series of quick, even steps that give the illusion of gliding across the stage. It can be done in any direction.

box step—The pattern that this 6-count social dance step makes on the floor is that of a box, or square, in 3/4 time. The leader starts with the left foot stepping forward. That is followed by a step to the side with the right foot and then a step with the left foot in to meet the right foot. The right foot then steps back, the left foot steps side, and the right foot steps in to meet the left. The follower begins with the right foot stepping backward and reverses the pattern.

callback—An audition that you are invited back to so that the production staff can look at you for a second time and gain a better understanding of who you are and what your talents and abilities are.

call board—A bulletin board in the theatre that contains contact information, rehearsal schedules, and notes from the production staff.

call time—The time that performers are asked to be at rehearsal or performance.

canon—A choreographic device in which dancers begin, perform, and end the same movement phrase at different times to create a rippling effect of movement.

cardiorespiratory fitness—How efficiently the heart and lungs work to deliver oxygen to the cells of the body.

Castle, Irene (1893–1969) and **Castle, Vernon** (1887–1918)—Wife and husband dance partners credited with helping to create ballroom dance and bringing it to the musical theatre stage.

cattle call—An audition that is open to everyone.

châinés—A series of consecutive, traveling turns.

Champion, Gower (1919–1980)—A director–choreographer known for his grand musical numbers that used set pieces and props and sometimes overshadowed the rest of the show.

chassé—A sliding step in which one foot chases the other.

choreographer—The person who creates dances by planning and arranging movements.

choreography—The use of movement in musical theatre productions to accompany music and dancing to enrich, embellish, and sometimes help define the story line.

closed position—A social dance position in which partners face each other. The man's left hand holds the woman's right hand. Palms are touching, and fingers and thumbs are loosely clasped around each other's hands. The man's right hand rests on the woman's back, cradling her left shoulder blade. The woman's left arm rests on top of the man's right arm, and her left hand rests gently on his right shoulder.

cold reading—Reading from a script without having previously seen the material.

Cole, Jack (1911–1974)—The first Broadway choreographer to use ethnic dance in musicals. He is known as the father of theatrical jazz dance.

concept musical—A theatrical production that revolves around a central idea or theme, first introduced by Jerome Robbins.

Connolly, Bobby (1897–1944)—Dance director who popularized tap dance and made tap the most popular stage and movie musical dance form from 1900 to 1930.

contractility—The ability of a muscle to shorten, pull on bones, and cause movement.

contraction—A position often used in jazz dance. The torso contracts inward so that the abdomen is hollowed out and the spine forms a C shape. The pelvis is pulled forward, but the shoulders remain over the hips.

contrast—An aesthetic principle that focuses on highlighting various parts of a dance to emphasize important movements and messages. This principle helps avoid monotony.

corporate musical—Theatrical productions produced and managed by entertainment corporations.

coupé—At the front or back of the ankle or middle of the lower leg.

cue—An indication that a change will occur, such as an entrance, an exit, a scene change, or a lighting change.

cue to cue—A rehearsal during which the actors move from cue to cue so that lighting and sound may be set.

dance captain—The choreographer's assistant who assists with teaching and rehearsing choreography.

dégagé—A brush to a pointed, stretched position of the foot about an inch (2.5 cm) from the floor.

de Mille, Agnes (1905–1993)—One of the most influential Broadway choreographers, she changed the role that dance played in musicals by creating the integration musical and hiring well-trained dancers.

demi-plié—A half bend of the knees in turned-out or parallel position of the feet.

demi-pointe—The heel of the foot is raised off the floor, and the dancer balances on the toes and metatarsals, or ball, of the foot.

développé—An unfolding of the leg in different directions at either 45 to 90 degrees or higher.

director—The person responsible for overseeing the development, creation, and production of a musical.

do si do—Used in folk or square dances, this figure begins with two dancers facing each other. They pass by each other right shoulder to right shoulder, pass each other back to back, and then return to their original positions by passing left shoulder to left shoulder. During a do si do, the dancers stay facing the same direction the entire time.

downstage—The front of the stage nearest the audience.

dress rehearsal—A complete rehearsal in full costume and makeup.

dry tech rehearsal—Only the technical crew is present to use the equipment.

dynamics—The intensity of the energy used during a movement.

dynamic stretching—Active stretching during which the body is constantly moving.

elasticity—The ability of a muscle or tendon to return to its original state after being stretched.

elevé—A rise to the toes and metatarsals, or ball, of the foot with straight legs.

excitability—The ability of a muscle to receive a message, or stimulus, from the brain and respond to it.

extensibility—The ability of a muscle to release and return to its relaxed state.

fan kick—In this kick, the working leg crosses in front of the body and arcs up to create a half circle before coming down on the opposite side.

Felix, Seymour (1892–1961)—The highest paid dance director of his time, he created dances that began to help tell the story of a musical.

flat back—In this position, you bend forward from the hips at a 90-degree angle and have the back straight and parallel to the floor. You should focus down and keep your neck in line with the rest of the spine.

flexed foot—A position in which the foot bends at the ankle, the arch of the foot is pulled toward the shin, and the toes extend upward.

flexibility—The range of motion that occurs at a joint.

flick—Moving the foot from a full-foot position to a pointed position in the air with a flicking motion to increase foot articulation.

focus—Where the dancer is looking when dancing.

forced arch—A rise to the toes and metatarsals, or ball, of the foot with a bent knee.

Fosse, Bob (1927–1987)—Director–choreographer known for his razzle-dazzle dance numbers that featured isolations, undulations, and percussive movements.

full-foot position—The entire foot is on the floor with the weight equally distributed between the toes, metatarsals, and the heel.

Glover, Savion (1973–)—Director–choreographer who worked to keep tap in musical theatre performances and directed Broadway's first hip-hop musical, *Bring in Da' Noise, Bring in Da' Funk*.

grand battement—A brush of the leg to a height of 90 degrees or higher.

grand jeté lift—The dancer being lifted begins with one leg in demi-plié, executes a leap forward, and lands on the other leg in a demi-plié. The dancer who is doing the lifting places his hands on the waist of his partner, demi-pliés, and lifts her as she leaps, supporting her and increasing the height of her jump.

grand plié—A full bend of the knees in turned-out or parallel foot position.

grapevine—A step in which one foot steps to the side and the other foot steps across in front of it. The original foot then steps to the side again, and the other foot steps across behind it. The pattern that it creates is that of grapevine growing. Each step receives half a count. The first cross in the grapevine can be either back or front.

heel and toe—The heel of one foot touches the floor and is followed by the toes of the same foot touching the floor. Used in folk dance.

high level—The space overhead that we occupy when we jump or stand on our toes.

hitch kick—A hitch kick begins in a lunge position. The back leg brushes forward, and as the dancer jumps into the air, the second leg brushes forward while the first leg is coming down for the dancer to land on in a demi-plié. During this jump, the legs pass each other in a scissor-like manner. A hitch kick may also be performed with the first leg coming to a bent position and the second leg brushing straight or to the back, with both legs brushing backward instead of forward.

house manager—The person responsible for the box office and everything that happens in the seating area and lobby of the theatre.

improvise—To act out a scene or situation spontaneously.

inside-hands joined position—The partners stand side by side. The man extends his right arm and offers his right hand to his partner, and the woman places her left palm in the man's right hand. Both place their outside hands on their hips.

integration musical—A musical play in which music, acting, and dance all work together to tell a story.

in the round—A performance on an arena stage that can be seen from all directions.

isolations—Keeping the body still while moving only certain parts like the head, shoulders, ribs, or hips.

jazz hands—The hands are opened wide so that the palms are facing the audience and the fingers are splayed open. Made popular by Bob Fosse.

jazz runs—Jazz walks that are done quicker and cover more distance with each step. The dancer should appear to be gliding across the floor.

jazz split—One leg extends in front of the body, and the back leg bends at the knee as the dancer slides to the floor.

jazz square—The feet trace the shape of a square on the floor. To do a jazz square to the left, the right foot crosses in front, the left foot steps back about 12 inches (30 cm) behind the right foot, the right foot steps 12 inches to the right of the left foot, and the left foot steps 12 inches in front of the right foot to complete the pattern. The step can be reversed by starting on the left foot.

jazz walks—These walks are similar to ballet walks in that on each step the dancer touches the floor first with the toe, rolls through the foot, and touches the heel on the floor last. Jazz walks are done in demi-plié with long strides. Arms are usually used in opposition so that when you are stepping forward with the right foot, the left arm is extended to the front and the right arm is extended to the back.

jeté—The literal translation is "thrown." A jeté is any leap that transfers weight from one leg to the other.

Jones, Bill T. (1952–)—Modern dancer and choreographer known for seamlessly weaving dance into the story line of musicals.

juke joint—A gathering place for music, dancing, and drinking run by African Americans for African Americans during the 1930s.

kinesphere—A bubble of space around the body, labeled by Rudolf Laban; personal space.

leap—A traveling jump that transfers weight from one foot to the other.

lighting designer—Uses lighting to ensure that all areas of the stage and the performers are visible at the right times, to set the mood, to direct the audience's attention, and to indicate the time of day during scenes.

load-in—Moving the set, hanging the lighting instruments, setting up the sound, and bringing in the costumes and props for a production.

low level—Close to the floor.

lunge—A position frequently used in jazz choreography. The weight is shifted onto one leg that is in demi-plié while the other leg is held straight.

mark—Going through dance movements quickly to help facilitate learning, using less energy than when actually performing the movements.

Marshall, Rob (1960–)—Mentored by Susan Stroman and known for his imaginative and new staging in the 1990s.

metabolism—The speed at which the body is able to convert food into energy.

middle level—The space that we move in on a daily basis.

minstrel shows—America's first musical shows that included cast members who sang, danced, and played instruments during the 1800s.

Mitchell, Julian (1854–1926)—He developed the idea of the production number and was one of Broadway's first choreographers, working on *Ziegfeld Follies*, *The Wizard of Oz*, and *Babes in Toyland*.

movement qualities—Describes how energy is applied to create a motion. The various qualities are sustained, percussive, swinging, vibratory, suspending, and collapsing.

muscle memory—The development and reinforcement of a neural pathway between a muscle and the brain that results in automatic movement patterns.

muscular endurance—The ability of a muscle or muscle group to contract repeatedly over time.

muscular imbalance—A condition in which certain muscles or groups of muscles are tighter or stronger than others.

muscular strength—The maximum force that a muscle or muscle group can exert.

musicality—Knowledge of and sensitivity to music.

music director—The person responsible for overseeing the teaching and playing of the music in a musical production.

negative space—The empty space between body parts or between people.

notes—Feedback from the director and choreographer to improve the production.

one-hand joined position—In social dance, the same as the two-hands joined position but each partner uses only one hand.

pas de bourrée—A step used to change weight from one foot to the other that can travel back, side, and front. For the basic pas de bourrée to the side, the left foot steps on relevé behind the right, the right steps on relevé to the right side, and the left foot closes full foot in front. The step is completed in two counts.

pas de chat—The cat step. If the dancer is traveling to the right, from demi-plié the right leg is lifted to a retiré back position. As this foot begins to return to the floor, the left leg lifts to a retiré front position before both feet sequentially land in the original position. When traveling to the left, the jump begins with the left foot. The step is executed in one count.

pathways—The patterns created on the floor as a dancer moves through the space.

personal space—The area surrounding a dancer; the kinesphere.

pique turn—In this turn the dancer steps onto demi-pointe on a straight leg and draws the other leg into a coupé or retiré position while turning. It can be executed in either a parallel or turned-out position. If it is done in a turned-out position, the coupé or retiré is placed behind the supporting leg.

pirouette—A turn on one leg in relevé.

pit orchestra—A group of musicians who play the music during performances of a musical.

pivot turn—Turn used to change the facing of the body. It can be executed as a quarter turn or a half turn. The working leg steps forward on the ball of the foot, and the supporting leg remains in place as the pivot point. The feet remain in this position as the body turns, rotating on the balls of the feet.

places—Cue the stage manager gives performers when they must get to where they need to be when the show begins.

pointed foot—A position in which the foot extends from the ankle as the arch lifts and the toes stretch.

polka—This three-step movement begins with a hop. Beginning with the weight on the right foot, the dancer hops on the right and then steps left, right, left. The step then reverses with the hop on the left foot and stepping right, left, right. It can travel in any direction and is counted "and 1, 2, 3 and 1, 2, 3." It is commonly used in folk dances.

port de bras—The carriage of the arms in ballet.

positive space—The space filled by the body.

PRICED method—A plan to follow immediately after an injury occurs that includes protecting the injured area from further injury, resting the injured area, applying ice to the injury, compressing the injured area, elevating the injury above the heart, and seeking a medical diagnosis.

producer—The person who oversees all parts of the production.

proscenium arch theatre—A theatre in which a raised stage is separated from the audience by an arch that frames the stage.

proteins—Molecules in the body that repair tissue damage.

Rausch, Albertina (1891–1967)—Dance director who combined elements of ballet with vaudeville dance and precision dancing and set it to modern music. Her New York school promoted strong training, and her students were known as the Albertina Rausch Girls.

read-through—A rehearsal at which all performers look at the script together for the first time and read through their parts.

relevé—A rise to the toes and metatarsals, or ball, of the foot that begins and ends with a demi-plié.

repetition—An aesthetic principle that focuses on recurring movements throughout the dance. Repetition provides a connection to the audience members instead of a constant bombardment of new sensory input.

retiré—A position in which one leg is bent and the toes are touching the front, back, or side of the other knee.

Robbins, Jerome (1918–1998)—Broadway choreographer who introduced the concept musical. Although classically trained, he researched the historical background for each of the musicals on which he worked to create ethnologically sound dances. The shows that he choreographed included *On the Town* (1944), *The King and I* (1951), *West Side Story* (1957), and *Fiddler on the Roof* (1964).

rock step—A rocking step in social dance that transfers the weight from one foot to the other. The dancer steps backward on one foot with a full transfer of weight and

wardrobe and makeup supervisor—The person in charge of costume and makeup design in a theatrical production.

Wayburn, Ned (1874–1942)—Founded the Studio of Stage Dancing in 1905 in Manhattan, New York. His dancers were trained in musical comedy dance, tap, acrobatics, ballet, and ballroom dance. He based his casting on appearance and was the first dance director to demand that all the dancers in his chorus line be the same size.

working leg—The leg that is gesturing or lifted into the air.

Ziegfeld, Florenz (1867–1932)—Broadway producer responsible for the *Ziegfeld Follies*, which was a musical revue produced annually from 1916 through 1919 and 1922 through 1923.

Ziegfeld Follies—A musical revue produced annually by Florenz Ziegfeld from 1916 through 1919 and again from 1922 through 1923.

References and Resources

Berkson, Robert. (1990). *Musical Theater Choreography: A Practical Method for Preparing and Staging Dance in a Musical Show*. New York: Backstage Books.

Bordman, Gerald. (1985). *American Musical Revue*. New York: Oxford University Press.

Bordman, Gerald. (2001). *American Musical Theatre: A Chronicle*. 3rd ed. New York: Oxford University Press.

Brantley, Ben. (2003, December 5). Tapping toward love in celebrated slippers. *New York Times*. www.nytimes.com.

Brantley, Ben. (2014, April 10). The chanteuse and the gun are loaded. *New York Times*. www.nytimes.com.

Brockett, Oscar G. (1988). *The Essential Theatre*. 4th ed. Chicago: Holt, Rinehart and Winston.

Driver, Ian. (2000). *A Century of Dance: A Hundred Years of Musical Movement From Waltz to Hiphop*. London: Octopus.

Engel, Lehman. (1957). *Planning and Producing the Musical*. New York: Crown.

Engel, Lehman. (1975). *The American Musical Theater*. New York: MacMillan.

Ganzl, Kurt. (2001). *The Encyclopedia of Musical Theatre*. New York: Schirmer Books.

Grant, Mark. (2004). *The Rise and Fall of the Broadway Musical*. Lebanon, NH: Northeastern University Press.

Green, Stanley. (1976). *Encyclopedia of the Musical*. London: Cassell.

Green, Stanley. (1990). *Hollywood Musicals: Year by Year*. Milwaukee, WI: Hal Leonard.

Hummer, David. (1984). *The Collector's Guide to the American Musical Theatre*. Metuchen, NJ: Scarecrow Press.

Isherwood, Charles. (2006, June 16). In "Spring Awakening," a rock 'n' roll heartbeat for 19th-century German schoolboys. *New York Times*. www.nytimes.com.

Isherwood, Charles. (2009, December 30). Cue the chorus: The musical endures. *New York Times*. www.nytimes.com.

Isherwood, Charles. (2012, August 1). High school rivalry, with a leg up. *New York Times*. www.nytimes.com.

Isherwood, Charles. (2013, November 3). Time travel and time steps: Tapping into Harlem history. *New York Times*. www.nytimes.com.

Kenrick, John. (2011). *Musical Theatre: A History*. New York: Continuum International.

Kislan, Richard. (1987). *Hoofing on Broadway*. New York: Prentice Hall Press.

Kraines, Minda Goodman, and Esther Kan. (1983). *Jump Into Jazz*. Palo Alto, CA: Mayfield.

Lerner, Alan Jay. (1986). *The Musical Theatre: A Celebration*. London: William Collins Sons.

Levine, Debra. (2012). *Jack Cole (1911–1974)*. Dance Heritage Coalition. www.danceheritage.org/treasures/cole_essay_levine.pdf.

Long, Robert Emmet. (2001). *Broadway, The Golden Years*. New York: Continuum International.

Moore, Tracey, and Allison Bergman. (2008). *Acting the Song*. New York: Allworth Press.

Miller, Scott. (2007). *Strike Up the Band*. Portsmouth, NH: Heinemann.

National Strength and Conditioning Association. (2008). *Essentials of Strength Training and Conditioning*. 3rd ed. Champaign, IL: Human Kinetics.

Norton, Richard C. (2002). *A Chronology of American Musical Theater*. New York: Oxford University Press.

Novak, Elaine A. (1988). *Performing in Musicals*. New York: Schirmer Books.

Novak, Elaine, and Deborah Novak. (1996). *Staging Musical Theatre*. Cincinnati, OH: Betterway Books.

Parker, Derek, and Julia Parker. (1975). *The Natural History of the Chorus Girl*. New York: Bobbs-Merrill.

Porter, Steven. (1997). *The American Musical Theatre: A Complete Musical Theatre Course*. Studio City, CA: Empire.

Slide, Anthony. (1994). *The Encyclopedia of Vaudeville*. Westport, CT: Greenwood Press.

Sunderland, Margot, and Ken Pickering. (1990). *Choreographing the Stage Musical*. New York: Theatre Arts Books.

Wright, Judy Patterson. (2013). *Social Dance Steps to Success*. 3rd ed. Champaign, IL: Human Kinetics.

Index

Note: The italicized *f* and *t* following page numbers refer to figures and tables, respectively.

About the Author

Diana Dart Harris has more than 24 years of experience teaching dance to students of all ages. She is a professor and musical theatre choreographer at the University of New Haven. She is trained in ballet, modern, jazz, and tap dance and has performed in musicals. Harris was artistic director of New Haven Ballet's Nutcracker and assistant director of a musical theatre organization. She is a board member of the Connecticut Dance Alliance. Harris earned a bachelor of arts degree in dance education from Goucher College and a master of science degree in exercise physiology from Southern Connecticut State University.

Perfect introductory guides for learning, performing, and viewing dance genres!

You'll find other outstanding
dance resources at

www.HumanKinetics.com

In the U.S. call 1.800.747.4457

Australia 08 8372 0999

Canada 1.800.465.7301

Europe . . . . . +44 (0) 113 255 5665

New Zealand 0800 222 062